Rocked by God

Teens' Experiences of God

Written and Compiled by Fr. Dave Pivonka, TOR
with Katrina J. Zeno

Scripture translations: The New American Bible and the New International Version

All scripture translations from the New American Bible unless otherwise noted.

2000 publication by:
Franciscan University Press
Franciscan University of Steubenville
1235 University Blvd.
Steubenville, Ohio 43952

Cover and book design: Lori Bortz Design
Photography: Alex Kim, Steve Zehler, Lori Bortz

ISBN 1-888462-03-5
UP 211

Let no one look down on you because of your youth, but be a

continuing example of love, faith, and purity to believers.

1 Timothy 4:12

Table of Contents:

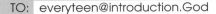

TO: everyteen@introduction.God

FROM: Father Dave

SUBJECT: **Introduction**

Has God ever rocked your world - you know, that experience where you're certain beyond a shadow of a doubt that God is real? What's that? You don't think you have been rocked? Well, you need to! And that is what this book is all about.

I remember when God rocked Jim's world. I had just finished speaking at a conference in Atlanta, Georgia, when Jim approached me. He was tough looking. You know the type: ball cap, Adidas T-shirt, jeans, dark hair, dark eyes. The eyes - I remember the eyes. They were glassy, kind of distant, kind of searching. He looked like he was going to cry. Jim asked if he could talk to me for a few minutes. We began walking and soon Jim began to slow down. He looked up, he looked at me, he looked through me, and asked, "Fr. Dave, why didn't anyone ever tell me that stuff?" "What stuff?" I asked. "All the stuff that you just told us, that sex before marriage was wrong, that pornography was wrong, that it was destructive." Tears ran down Jim's cheeks. "Why didn't anyone ever tell me that there was a God who was passionately in love with me, a God who would forgive me?"

God had rocked Jim's world, and he would never be the same.

Today, right now, God is rocking a lot of people's worlds, especially teens through Franciscan University's youth conferences. Since 1996 when I began working with the youth conferences, teens from all over the country and Canada have enthusiastically told me about God rocking their world. With each letter or e-mail I received, I wished others could read these experiences. I knew there were thousands, even millions, of teens (and adults) who could benefit from reading these stories. Stories of faith. Stories of forgiveness. Stories of freedom.

Then one day as I was praying, I had an inspiration (imagine that): "Other teens could read these if you *published* them." Hmmm. So in the summer of 1999 I encouraged teens to send me their stories. These are what follow.

As you read these stories I hope you will experience the incredible freedom and healing that comes from a personal relationship with Jesus Christ. I want you to know that you can experience the power of God in the Catholic Church. I want you to know that you are not alone, that there are teens all over this country just like you.

I BELIEVE IN YOU. I believe you hear God, that you experience God, that you are able to know truth and embrace it. I believe you can live as a faithful Catholic Christian. I believe your life can challenge the world and change the culture. I believe the world can learn from you and be inspired by you. I believe your story will help others know God's forgiveness and love.

You have something to offer the church. You are needed precisely because you are young. Your youth is not an obstacle, but something to be celebrated, something to be lived.

This book is for you because it is from you. Thank you for sharing not only your stories with me but your very selves. Both are sacred. I will forever remember you in my thoughts, prayers, and Masses. I love you, and I pray that God will continue to **rock your world.**

*Fr. Dave Pivonka, TOR

Warning....Warning....Read this before going any further. This book could be hazardous to your world.

Did I get your attention? Good, because before you jump into these awesome stories, I want to prep you for what you're going to encounter.

First off, you're going to see some names in these stories. Are they the real names? Sorry...they're not. At first, I thought it would be fun for teens to see their names in print, but then I realized that some of these stories are *so* revealing, *so* personal, that anonymity was important. Therefore, you know the famous line: "All the names have been changed to protect the innocent."

Secondly, you may be wondering: What in the world is a Franciscan University Youth Conference?

I'm glad you asked!! The youth conferences are *the* place to be for any teen in the summer. The conferences begin on Friday evening and conclude with Mass on Sunday morning. In between, teens encounter a living God. This is not a ho-hum, I'm-an-old-man-with-a-beard kind of God. This is a rockin' God who shows up through dynamic preaching, lively music, and powerful sacraments. Throughout the weekend, teens are invited to enter into a personal relationship with Jesus Christ and experience God's healing love.

The conferences build to a Holy Hour with Eucharistic adoration (also called exposition and benediction) on Saturday evening. During the Holy Hour the priest processes among the teens with the Blessed Sacrament displayed in a monstrance (that's a beautiful gold holder that looks like a sunburst). God's power breaks forth and teens experience some amazing things (you'll read about these): the gift of tears ("I bawled my eyes out"), the gift of laughter ("I couldn't keep from laughing; it felt so good!"), the gift of faith ("As soon as I saw the Eucharist, I knew it was Jesus"), and being slain in the Spirit ("I fell to the ground and couldn't get up"). On Sunday morning, the teens are encouraged to keep the fire burning and to share what they have experienced with their family and friends at home. The conference concludes with the celebration of the Eucharist, and let me tell you, it's some celebration!

So where do you go to attend one of these things? Well, it used to be that everyone had to travel to Steubenville, Ohio, because we only had **one** conference. But by 1994, over 3,400 youth were showing up and more wanted to come. Have you ever tried to keep track of 3,400 teens at once? Crazy. So we split the conference into two, and the next year, we offered our first off-campus youth conference in Alexandria, Louisiana. The word got out that God was doing awesome things at these conferences, and by 1999, we were offering eleven youth conferences with over 20,000 teens attending.

Here's where you can check them out - on our website

(www.franciscanyouth.com) or in person: Steubenville, Ohio; Attleboro, Massachusetts (Steubenville East); Tucson, Arizona (Steubenville West); Atlanta, Georgia (Steubenville Atlanta); Alexandria, Louisiana (Steubenville South); Denver, Colorado (Steubenville of the Rockies); St. Louis, Missouri (Steubenville St. Louis); and South Bend, Indiana (Steubenville South Bend). You'll also notice that many teens come back for more (even five times!) and some become involved as "young apostles," serving their peers during the conference.

What's the secret to this youth explosion? It's simple: we provide the space and time for teens to encounter God, and God shows up. But enough of my blabbing. Let's get on to the good stuff. Fasten your seat belt and get ready for God to rock *your* world!

TO: everyteen@love.God

FROM: Father Dave

SUBJECT: **God's Love**

What if you were five or six, and I asked you to write a letter to Jesus, what would you say? One little boy on a retreat I led in Cleveland wrote this: "Dear God, I need more love. Johnny." Tears came to my eyes as I read his letter. Children who are five shouldn't know they need more love. But wait, isn't this ultimately what life is all about? We *all* need more love - more of God's love.

God loves you. He has a passion for you. He is deeply and madly in love with you. This isn't, "Oh, I love Jimmy sooooooo much. He's sooooooo cute." It isn't a cloud-nine, crush type of love. This is real love. It is total. It is complete. It's laying down one's life for another. This is the love God has for you.

The next time you watch a football game, look for the sign in the crowd that says "John 3:16." Do you know what that verse says? It says: "God so loved the world that he gave his only Son, that whoever believes in him may not die, but may have eternal life." That's LOVE in a nutshell: 1) God loves; 2) He loves you so much He sent His son; 3) His son loved you so much He died for you; 4) This Love wants you to be with Him forever.

Sometimes I ask my students at Franciscan University to say this verse and insert their own name. Try it. "God so loves _____ (your name) that he gave his only Son, that if _____ believes in Him _____ may not die but may have eternal life."

Many people believe God loves the whole world, but have a hard time believing that God loves them. God does not love generally. He loves specifically. You are not just one of the crowd. You are unique. You are original AND GOD LOVES YOU!! There is nothing you can do to make him love you *more*. There is nothing you can do to make him love you *less*. (Think that one over for awhile!)

If God can't love us any more or less, then there's nothing we can do to ever cause God to stop loving us. Romans 8:35 makes this quite clear: "What will separate us from the love of Christ? Will anguish, or distress, or persecution, or famine, or nakedness, or peril, or the sword? No, in all these things we conquer overwhelmingly through him who loved us. For I am convinced that neither death, nor life, nor angels, nor principalities, nor present things, nor future things, nor powers, nor height, nor depth, nor any other creature will be able to separate us from the love of God in Christ Jesus our Lord."

God's love is a gift. It's free. You can't earn it or deserve it.

It doesn't matter if you're the greatest saint or sinner who ever lived. God loves you the same. He can't love you more. He simply loves. Ohhhhhh, but of course, YOU can do things (sin) that stop YOU from *experiencing* God's love. But, that doesn't mean He has stopped loving you. He still loves you as much right now as He ever will, which is entirely, passionately, and perfectly. (Are you getting the point?)

Some of you may be saying, "Father Dave, you don't know what I've done." You're right. I don't know, but it doesn't matter. God knows, and He loves you just the same. This is the most important point of this book: God loves you. It's all about His love. When you come to understand this, when you experience HIS love, then life is never the same.

Your Experiences of God's Love

When I arrived at Franciscan University, I wasn't thankful to be there, I was just glad to get out of the van! At that point, I was worried about recently losing my job, where I would get money, finding a better car, and most of all, about finding a girlfriend. I was depressed and feeling like no one loved me. I felt even God didn't love me.

Saturday night I was proved wrong. When Christ passed by me during Eucharistic adoration, I broke down in tears - tears of joy and sorrow. I can't explain how He did it, but I felt God's embrace and heard His voice as He used a friend to tell me I am loved. I believe God was talking to me because I never told this friend I was depressed, but she told me what God knew I needed to hear.

Even though God showed how He loved me, I was not satisfied in how I showed my love for Him. Until then, I had never truly given God what He wanted - my life-long devotion. Regretfully, Friday night when we were given the chance to stand and give ourselves to the Lord, I had remained seated; something held me back. However, after what I felt Saturday night, nothing was going to hold me back on Sunday. As soon as the offer to stand was given, up I went. Standing with my eyes closed, I prayed my life into God's hands. As I prayed, I saw in my mind a fire engulf me and thousands of faces cheering. I believe it was the fire of the Holy Spirit and all the souls of heaven. Thanks be to God for all His wondrous gifts!
Signed,
I Got More Than Just a Van Ride

Dear "More than Just a Van Ride,"
God is sooooooo good! You're right - all God wants is our life. We give him our messed-up, confused lives and He gives us His life in return, a

life filled with His love and peace. What a great trade!! Keep "praying your life" into His hands and letting the fire of God's love engulf you.
✝ Fr. Dave

I didn't want to go to the Steubenville youth conference AT ALL, but I was forced to go to fulfill confirmation requirements. I was not looking forward to a 16-hour bus ride, but the ride ended up being as good as the conference itself!

At the conference, I accepted God into my life for the first time, and God began to work in me and through me. However, my first experience at Steubenville was nothing compared to the next few years. It was just enough to get me to go back for more and more, and to become involved in my church.

The best things about my five youth conferences, besides bringing me to the Lord, was providing a place where I always felt I belonged. I never fit in at school and did not have many friends, but whenever I went to Steubenville I had friends there, and I felt loved. Because of this love - because it was God's love - I was able to grow as a person and to make it through the hard times in my life when I felt I had no friends and that no one liked me, let alone loved me.

Now I am in college, and I have become more outgoing and less shy. I am a cantor at school and at home. I would never have done that in high school. I was too afraid. The Steubenville conferences helped me grow by helping me find God and receive His love.
Signed,
Five Timer

Dear "Five Timer,"
Five conferences - heck, you should come work for me! I'm right with you when you talk about finding a place where you belong. We *all* need to belong. God placed that need within us because He wants us to belong to Him. It's awesome how you allowed God's love to get you through the hard times. Let go and let God! ✝ Fr. Dave

When I first heard about the Steubenville youth conference at Notre Dame, I didn't think it would be all that thrilling. But, by Saturday morning, I was enjoying it greatly. The men's session changed me a lot. By Sunday, I was already getting along much better with my dad. The conference also showed me not to be scared of God because He loves you a lot and would never hurt you.
Signed,
Thrilled

Dear "Thrilled,"
You got that right - God is not going to hurt us. However, isn't it odd how many people are afraid that He will? We need to pray for more trust. This doesn't mean that bad things will never happen to us, but that He is going to walk with us and continue to love us through them.
✝ Fr. Dave

I used to rely on retreats to form my relationship with Christ. I guess you could call me a "retreat Catholic." It wasn't until 1999 and my fifth Steubenville youth conference that I realized that my relationship with Christ comes through prayer. Prayer was always too difficult for me because I never had time or I couldn't concentrate. When I did pray, I prayed for the things I thought I needed, and never realized that maybe I didn't really need them and that was why I wasn't getting them.

At my fifth conference, I needed some peace and prayed God would give me peace. Well, since God is in control, He said NO! He saw that I was unhappy for so many years and He said that what I needed was joy. God gave me what I needed rather than what I wanted.

I thank God endlessly for giving me such joy. I came home and smiled so much, I think it's permanent. God loves me so much, and it took me five conferences to realize that.
Signed,
Smiley

Dear "Smiley,"
Retreat Catholics, or as I like to call them - conference junkies - go from retreat to retreat and conference to conference looking for spiritual highs. Then, when times get tough (and they will), their faith often falls apart. What they need is to be grounded in God, not just a feeling or experience. What they need is prayer, daily prayer. This anchors us in God's love so that even when the winds around us are turbulent we won't sink because we know that God is still in charge. Hope that smile is still there! ✝ Fr. Dave

In 1999, I served as a young apostle at one of Franciscan University's youth conferences. Since I'd been before, I figured I knew what to expect. But, like always, God had more in store for me than I could ever imagine!!!

On Saturday night I expected to feel a flood of emotions - regret, guilt, fear, love, and finally hope. This time, however, something was different. I had gone to confession and the priest told me to ask God to show me the outpouring of His love.

During the Holy Hour on Saturday night, I began praying for our youth ministry and my friends. As I prayed over my best friend, words began to come out of my mouth: "God loves you, let Him take you completely. He forgives you, forgive yourself." These words were not my own. I believe God used me to touch her.

Another boy in our youth ministry was having difficulties with drugs and how they were separating him from his parents. I prayed that God would open his eyes to the problems the drugs were causing. Finally, he said to me: "I need to make up with my parents. Drugs are ruining my life." That's exactly what I was praying for!

At Mass on Sunday, we were asked to open our hands to accept the gifts God wanted to give us. I had almost forgotten about the priest's suggestion to pray for the outpouring of God's love. I felt a tight, burning sensation in my chest, and soon it was in the palms of my hands. I just sat there, smiling so big. I knew God was showing me His love, the outpouring of His love, and the feeling in my hands was Jesus showing me what He did for me on the cross. I sat there for so long not wanting that feeling to leave. The fire went away, but the feeling of love, the outpouring of love, didn't.
Signed,
Always More

Dear "Always More,"
You are tremendous! You keep coming back for more because God always has more for us! His love is as big as an ocean and we are like small buckets. It's impossible to pour the whole ocean into a little bucket, but God keeps trying. Aren't you glad? ✝ Fr. Dave

(Hey, don't skip the long ones. They're worth it!)

The first time I went to a Steubenville youth conference, I didn't believe in God, heaven, or hell. All my life I had been looking for someone to love me, even though I never admitted it to myself. My parents divorced when I was two months old, and my mom raised me and my four older sisters by herself for two years before remarrying. I never felt that my step-dad loved me, and I never looked at him as a father figure. My real father lived in Florida while my family and I lived in Texas. I only saw him twice a year and never felt that he loved me.

I always thought I was the reason for my parents' divorce. My older sisters were into drugs and alcohol, even though my mom, dad, and step-dad never drank. When my mom was at work, my older sisters had to watch me, and they took me with them while they did drugs and got into fights. Finally my mom and step-dad decided to move us out to Indiana, to get away from the city and to make sure that my one older sister and I didn't get into the same lifestyle as my other sisters.

I was always a good kid. I always prayed and was nice to everyone. But a week after Christmas of my freshman year in high school, my dad died of leukemia. I talked to him just a few days before Christmas, and for some reason when I hung up, I didn't tell him that I loved him. I always told him, "I love you," but this time I didn't. Maybe it was because I kept telling myself that he wouldn't die, because dads don't do stuff like that.

The night of his funeral, my cousin took me out with her friends and they taught me how to inhale a cigarette. I thought I was so cool hanging out with people from the east coast and learning how to smoke. I had taken puffs of people's cigarettes, but had never inhaled until then. My freshman year, I drank a lot, but only at parties. Then, during the summer after my freshman year, I started drinking even more. I had my first taste of Vodka. I thought it was so good that I drank over half the bottle and my boyfriend had the other half. Well, everyone knows that when you get drunk you do a lot of stupid things. I had sex with my boyfriend that night. I was 15. At the time I thought I was so old, but now I realize how young I really was.

Even though I drank, I swore up and down that I would never smoke pot. All the teachers told us that drinking was the gateway to drugs, and I thought, yeah, right…. Sophomore year came around, and I wanted so desperately to be in with the popular crowd. Everyone knew that the popular crowd did drugs. So I started smoking pot and denied the real reason why I smoked: I wanted love. If I smoked pot, I felt good and the guys noticed me.

I started smoking pot only at parties. Then it was "just on the weekends," which led to every day, and then to many times a day. I got drunk constantly, but to me it didn't seem like it was enough. The popular guys were always calling me and my friends in the middle of the night, asking us to sneak over, which we did. Everyone always snuck out and went to David's house where there were always drugs to smoke and beer to drink. I had a huge crush on David, and he knew it. We would get high and then fool around. This happened every weekend throughout my entire sophomore year. I was considered David's girl even though he never talked to me at school.

I was completely depressed because I couldn't get him to go out with me. But at the same time it didn't bother me to have him never talk to me at school and to only ask me to mess around with him. My best bud was always messing around with one of his friends, and it didn't bother her either. One of our friends asked us how we could stand to mess around with a guy we really liked and then have him completely ignore us at school. We both said, "You get used to it." And you do. You get numb to the pain, to the hurt, to the stares, and to the gossip.

I went to school high almost everyday. I always had someone to drive me to school who had weed. On the way home from school we would get high again. My grades totally fell, but it didn't matter to me. Nothing mattered to me. I was a total bitch to my family and people at school. No one seemed to care about what I was doing, so I kept on doing it.

For an entire week I went to school drunk. I couldn't even stand upright. I got called into the disciplinarian's office about a rumor that I had been bringing alcohol to school, which I denied and got away with.

My self esteem was totally gone. I felt that God had abandoned me. Then I finally decided that he didn't exist. If he existed, then how could he let me feel so bad about myself, how could he let my dad die, and how could he let no guy like me for me? All the guys just wanted to have sex with me, and I let a few of them get what they wanted. Every time I had sex I was drunk.

After I decided that there was no God, I felt completely empty inside. I constantly wrote poems about death, asking to die. I wanted to die. I cried all the time for reasons that I didn't understand. I started to hurt myself physically. I burned my arm several times. The scars are still there. I told people they were from curling irons and stoves. I let people read my poems and instead of getting people to feel sorry for me and give me help (which was what I wanted), I got nothing. No one cared because they thought I was trying to get attention, which I was, but high schoolers don't care about people who try to get attention.

By the end of my sophomore year, I was a depressed girl looking for love, a pothead, and a person who didn't believe in God. My mom decided to send me to the youth conference at Steubenville. I almost died. I did not want to go to a place full of holy rollers who dressed funny, just to hear about someone who didn't exist. My older sisters (who had turned their lives around) had gone to college there, and one still lived there.

So I went to my sister's house for the summer, and when she brought me to the youth conference there were tons of hotties. I thought, "Hey, this weekend is going to be awesome even if I have to listen to a bunch of crap." Well, God had other plans for me. I got what I wanted - an awesome guy to love me, but not in the way that I thought. The awesome guy was Jesus!!!!

I was still skeptical about Jesus, but I did believe in His presence. Saturday night of the conference was a night like no other. People started crying and laughing, and I didn't understand why. Someone told me to just pray, so I did and I felt so horrible for all the things that I had done. How could I have done any of that stuff? I bawled my eyes out. I asked for forgiveness and received it. I said that I was not going to drink, smoke pot or have sex anymore. I was totally ready to tell the world about Jesus. I even bought a Jesus T-shirt.

I got back to my sister's house and met another guy. This guy was the guy I was going to marry. He told me so. This is another whole story in itself, so I won't go into it, but he abused me mentally, we had sex many times each day, and did drugs together. Everything that had happened to me at the youth conference was gone, completely. I still believed in God, but only a little bit. I didn't believe that God cared about me.

I kept a long-distance relationship with this guy for six months. He eventually quit calling me. I was totally depressed and lonely again. I smoked pot frequently, but not every day. This lasted my entire junior year, until I went back to Steubenville.

This time something totally incredible happened to me. Friday night I went to confession and cried as I confessed my sins. Then I cried for an hour solid afterwards. I felt total sadness for how I had lived my life. Saturday night came and again I cried for what seemed an eternity. As the priest came by holding the monstrance with the host, I looked up and felt Jesus inside of me. I cried so hard. I cried out all my pain, anger, and sorrow that night. Then I felt incredibly happy. I started laughing uncontrollably. I couldn't help it. I felt like a weirdo, but I was finally happy!!!!

Then I prayed and asked the lady next to me to pray over me. She did and the next thing I knew, I was on the ground with people looking at me and asking me questions. I couldn't hear them, yet I knew what they were saying. I felt total peace in my soul. I couldn't move my body at all; I couldn't even talk. I felt as if something heavy had been dropped on me and I was stuck, but it felt good.

It was the Holy Spirit who came upon me and told me everything was okay, that God forgives me, Jesus loves me, and so does my Daddy (in heaven).

Sunday morning, I was asked to witness in front of 2,700 people. I have never felt so happy in all my life. I felt forgiven and loved all together. I felt like hugging everyone and telling them that God loves them and He forgives them because He does.

Drugs and sex don't make you feel good. They make you feel worse, and they don't bring you love and satisfaction. Even though at the time you'll swear that it does, if you look at yourself and write down how you're feeling, you'll see that you aren't happy with yourself. Until I let God take over my life, I was in complete denial about my feelings. I was out of control, and I was on my way to hell where you feel hurt and anger and that no one loves you. I couldn't stand that feeling on earth, and I sure as heck don't want to feel that way for all eternity.

Signed,

Lookin' for Love in All the Wrong Places

Dear "Lookin' for Love,"
Your sentence, "You get numb to the pain, to the hurt, to the stares, and to the gossip," really tore my heart. It's amazing what you can live with, what you can get used to. I believe this "numbness" is overwhelming for many teens. You don't know what to feel, or you simply can't feel. I have spoken with teens whose hurt is so great, so real, they simply have to turn it off. They can't take the pain so they get lost in drugs, alcohol, or bad relationships - anything just to numb the pain for awhile. But Jesus didn't come so that we may be numb. He came so that we may have LIFE, and have it to the full (John 10:10). Unfortunately, too many people think that the way they feel is the way life is. Thank God that He broke into your life and showed you that you don't have to feel numb. You can feel loved. I pray you will know this love each and every day, and then for all eternity in heaven.
✝ Fr. Dave
P.S. Tons of hotties??? I'm not even going to go there....

Prayer
Jesus, at times it's hard for me to believe that I am loved. I see all of the bad things I have done. I know sometimes I have failed you and not lived the way I should. Help me to really believe that I am loved by you. Help me to know that your love is stronger than my weakness. I believe that only your love can really give meaning to my life. Fill me with your love.

TO: everyteen@conversion.God

FROM: Father Dave

SUBJECT: **Conversion**

You've probably heard the word "conversion" before, but what does it mean? Simply put, it means doing a 180. It means turning from sin to God.

Some people make conversion sound like a one-time deal. Wrong. Conversion is something that happens time and time again. I need conversion. You need conversion. We all need conversion.

Think about it, in a normal day you have many opportunities for conversion. You can ignore someone who isn't in your group of friends or talk to them. You can cheat or be honest. You can go to the party where you *know* everyone will be drinking or you can stay away. You can be nice to your little sister or you can drive her crazy. Big, small, in between - the opportunities for conversion are endless.

But, before we get to the daily conversion stuff, many of us need a swift kick in the you-know-what. We need more than just a nudge or a whisper in the ear. We need a lightning bolt. We need something to happen so that we know, beyond a shadow of a doubt, that God is real. We need God to rock our world.

These are major conversion moments. These are the "God-is-real-and-now-I-know-that-He-forgives-me-and-loves-me-and-will-always-be-with-me" moments. One of my conversion moments happened in 1985. I spent this year with the National Evangelization Teams (NET), an organization devoted to evangelizing Catholic youth. On the first night, a staff member told me there was a prayer meeting, and I was welcome to attend. I thought it would be a good idea. It had been a long day and a little quiet time would be nice.

WRONG. As soon as the first song was over people began shouting and raising their hands and going nuts. (At least that's how it seemed to *me*.) I didn't know what was going on. I felt uncomfortable, like an outsider. However, I did notice that all of the people in the room were young and they were ALL excited about God.

The next day a guy from Washington asked me when I was baptized in the Holy Spirit. I didn't know exactly what he meant. I said I was baptized as a baby. "No, not baptized like the sacrament, but baptized in the Holy Spirit," he said. "When did people pray over you and you came to know the power of God and the Holy Spirit?" I didn't know what to say, but I was quite sure I hadn't experienced it. He looked at me with this look that reminded me of the witch in the Wizard

of Oz, "I'll get you, my pretty." Then he said to me, "Well, we need to pray over you."

Soon after, I realized these people had something I didn't. They seemed so alive, so real, so excited about God. A fire burned in them that was both attractive and scary. I was certain the Holy Spirit had something to do with it, and I began to want what they had.

One evening I was alone in the chapel. It was late. I was praying like I had never prayed before. I was pouring out my heart to God, telling Him that I wanted Him in my life and that I needed Him. I remember saying, "God, I don't know what this baptism in the Holy Spirit thing is all about, but if you want this for me I want it." FROM THAT MOMENT MY LIFE HAS NEVER BEEN THE SAME.

As I look back, I see this moment as one of the most significant events in my life. No one prayed over me. Great music wasn't playing. Eucharistic exposition wasn't occurring. It was just me and God and my saying YES to whatever He wanted. I felt the presence of God and His Holy Spirit like I never had before. I felt a fire. I *felt* truly alive. I *was* truly alive.

We all need conversion moments like this. St. Paul was rocked by God on the way to Damascus. (Remember his lightning bolt? Check out Acts 9:3-5.) However, not all conversions are accompanied by thunder, lightning, and voices from heaven, but ALL deep, authentic conversions are personal and real. We need to have an experience of God that changes us, turns us around, flips us upside down, and shakes us. When this happens, we can look back later and say, "There, that's when God did it! That's when He rocked my world."

One time a teen asked me how to know when this happens. Believe me, you'll know! If Michael Jordan walked into your room, you'd know, right? The same is true of God. When He walks into your life, you'll know.

God desires to make Himself known to you. He desires to be a personal God. We need to open the door of our hearts to Him. We need to ask Him to let us know He is real. We need to pray to be rocked by God.

Your Experiences of Conversion

As a sophomore in high school, I began to go out with a group of friends I had known since grade school. This group, you could say, was the "wrong group" because my life consisted of boys, beer, and seeing how much we could drink and being proud of that.

Then, at one of the Steubenville conferences, I felt God telling me that in order to live a good, Christian life, I would have to give this up. My first reaction was, "What? Give up alcohol and all the partying? Forget it!!" But, as time went on, I began to think about what God said. I had been trying to fill a void in my life with alcohol, and it didn't make me happy. I noticed, however, that God gave me a joy that I had never felt before. I decided I was going to change and my attitude toward drinking became totally different.

At my second Steubenville weekend, I experienced Jesus' deep love for me. As a result, I now have to climb over an uncomfortable wall: I need to find another healthier group of friends, and I need to share the love Jesus has shown me with my old group of friends. It would be much easier to leave them without saying a word, but it would be a shortcoming on my part. God gave me this experience not just for myself, but to share with others. I love my friends, and I can't just let them sin without trying to help them know the truth. Jesus is the truth, and He is the only thing that will give them eternal life and true happiness. God has changed my life little by little, and I know that I am on my way to His house in heaven.
Signed,
Wall Climber

Dear "Wall Climber,"
What a great work God has done in your life! After encountering God, many teens find it agonizing to separate themselves from "friends" who lead them away from God. This is often one of the most difficult things to do, and at times the most important. You realized this was necessary in order to really follow God. You've got courage!! But don't look at it like you are abandoning your friends. You're not abandoning your friends, in fact you may be doing the best thing for them. Continue praying for them and letting them SEE what God has done in your life. Keep climbing toward heaven because it's worth every bump and bruise! ✝ Fr. Dave

When I got on the bus at 11 p.m. on Thursday, July 30, 1998, I was ready for another typical retreat experience. You know, getting to hang out on a college campus and sneak out of those boring sessions to meet guys? Yeah, *those* retreats. Every retreat I'd attended in eighteen years had been like that. Why would this retreat, the first Catholic retreat I'd ever been to, be different??? Duh, it wouldn't be!

We arrived at Steubenville and "moved" into the dorm rooms. By then, at least, I was on speaking terms with people other than my mom and my brother. I was still not thrilled because it was going to be hard to meet cute guys and to find the people I was going to sneak out of the sessions with in such a huge ocean of 3,000 people. But, as the other girls and I worked up the nerve to approach random strangers, I realized this retreat would be different. Everyone had such an awesome array of interests and talents and seemed to be *alive*, as if they were ready and willing to be in Steubenville.

Then it was time for the first session. Great, three hours of sitting in a chair and singing ultra-happy, "we-are-trying-too-hard-to-be-in-the-nineties" songs. Gag me.

Okay, so now is where I say: BOY, WAS I EVER WRONG! There I was, sitting in a tent filled to the brim with 3,000 kids - *kids* - who were on their feet, clapping, singing, laughing, cheering, and screaming for Jesus so loudly you could swear the whole world was listening. No, this certainly had never happened at those other retreats, which reminded me of Chuck E. Cheese. No, we were at Red Lobster - this was fine dining!

No one was scanning the crowd for the hottest guy. No one was constantly fixing their hair, chewing their nails, or rolling their eyes or crossing their arms. Oh no, their arms were reaching up toward the sky, ready to be touched by the Holy Spirit. Just picture it: 3,000 kids, that's 6,000 arms, waving in the air. It was AWESOME. And it was only Friday night.

By the end of the first session, they asked those who wanted to give their lives to Jesus to stand. The Holy Spirit knocked the wind out of me when all around us kids started standing up - friends, strangers, adults. They were crying, bowing their heads, and then we started to sing. We sang and sang, and everyone was crying. We sang out to God for these brave souls whose lives were being changed right before our eyes. I could've stood there all night long, crying and singing.

I left that tent smiling, laughing, and floored by all that I was just catching a glimpse of. My friends and I ventured out into the cool and powered nighttime air and just started talking. We talked to everyone we met because suddenly everyone was so much closer. Every single person was beautiful, wonderful, and kind. No one was mean. No one was vain. No one was judgmental in any way.

It was extremely intense. The speakers had talked about the hard-core stuff - the crucifixion, the presence of the Holy Spirit, and all the things that require an unbelievable faith just to take in. The speakers hadn't presented the Catholic faith in lighter terms, politically correct terms, or in any manner that was different than it has been for 2,000 years. And THAT was what all these kids were crying about: They'd heard the Truth, the Tradition, the power of a faith that has remained unchanged by laws or generation X or feminists or liberals for 2,000 years. Phew, and all this in the first night.

I won't go into the wonderful details of the next day - about waking up excited for Mass or going to breakfast with thousands of smiling faces. And I'm sure you don't need to hear me go into depth about the electricity in the tent when 3,000 teenagers dropped to their knees before the Body and Blood of our Lord Jesus Christ during Mass. I'm sure you've been blessed to witness such an earth-trembling moment. Oh, wait, maybe you haven't. I hadn't either, since no one in our church kneels for the consecration during Mass.

Well, my fingers can't type fast enough so I can't linger on the coolness of Mass otherwise I'll never get to the rest of the second day!

The afternoon sessions were unbelievable. The women's session changed my outlook on almost everything about being female in the church, on the importance of saving my body and myself for my husband, and of all the things that girls are often shielded from in order to gender-neutralize the world and the church. It was AWESOME.

That day, I also stood in line for confession - a 90-minute wait to cleanse my soul. I stood in line with kids who smoked cigarettes, dyed their hair, pierced their tongues, and who wore black clothes and had dog collars around their necks. They talked about parties, boyfriends, sports, and their favorite bands, and then they entered the confession tent. They walked alone, willingly, after 1 1/2 hours in the blazing sunshine, into the confession tent and confessed all of their sins and purified their souls. It must have looked like a continuous cloud of forgiven sins being flung out of Steubenville.

Then nighttime arrived. SATURDAY night and all 3,000 of us were sitting in our seats waiting for the anticipated event: Eucharistic adoration. We listened to a couple of speakers, sang, and prepared ourselves for the hour that we would have to adore and worship Jesus, to be able to see His Body and know that He was there.

Then it was time. We all got down on our knees. The monstrance came in. I can't describe the following hour. I just can't. I knelt on the dirty, rocky ground for an hour. I knelt with 3,000 kids and wept at the sight of my Lord's Body. There He was, and who was I to be able to see Him and have Him love me?

I was overcome with love for that hour. I could feel my soul rejoicing. Our souls got to spend one hour with their eternal Beloved. They got to be near the One that they will love forever, and they were overcome with love and agony all at once. You could hear 3,000 souls crying out as they brought the monstrance around. For there before them was the One that they were created for and the One that they are impatiently waiting to be with. And only for an hour.

I watched teenagers being slain in the Spirit. They fell to the ground. Their souls absorbed the bombardment of love coming from Jesus. I closed my eyes and listened to the weeping, sobbing, and crying out for God. I heard laughter - the gift of joy - unstoppable laughter, loud and continuous at the sight of Jesus Christ.

You try and tell me this wasn't real. At that moment, I knew Truth. My body was a temple for my soul whose Lover was there before me, and I felt myself fall into the background as my soul shared these moments with the Love of its existence. And it was all real. Teenagers with dyed hair and pierced lips and baggy jeans don't fall to the ground and weep and laugh uncontrollably just BECAUSE. Oh, no, no, no, no. If you only could have seen it.

It changed my life. It changed everyone's lives. The only emotion that existed for the rest of the night and the weekend was joy, relief, and love.

But it had to end. Even though we didn't want to leave, the conference was over the next morning. Again we celebrated Mass. Again we sang together, and again we fell to our knees before our Eucharistic Lord. And we watched as hundreds of guys and girls who felt vocations to serve Jesus for the rest of their human lives stood up and went to the front. HUNDREDS OF KIDS. It brought the priests to tears. Then it was time to go.

When I got on the bus at noon on Sunday, August 2, 1998, I was a different person. I had changed for my Savior and for my church. No one can tell me that my faith is wrong or that Jesus is only a prophet, or even worse, that He doesn't exist. He exists. He is alive and well, and He is waiting for the rest of the world to come to Him with the same intensity and passion as the teenagers at Steubenville.
Signed,
Blew My Mind

Dear "Blew My Mind,"
Gidddy up! God sure had something in store for you. You went into the weekend thinking it would be boring and you came out of it with your life totally changed. So much for your plans... It's a shame so many teens think retreats or conferences have to be boring. God, boring? I'm sure He would have something to say about that. You see, we put God in this box and say, "this is how God is" or "this is how God works," and then God smashes these boxes and our lives are never the same. Thanks for letting God out of the box by opening your mind and heart to Him. ✝ Fr. Dave

When I was younger, I had a very close relationship with God. I was on fire for the Lord. Over the past two years, I started falling away from God. My life hit rock bottom in October of 1998 when I was arrested and spent two days in juvenile jail. Then my dad moved to Oregon, and I went with him.

Even though my dad knew I had hardened my heart and was angry with God, he kept me going to church. I started going to Life Teen at St. John's Catholic Church, and that's when my life started to turn around. That's where I heard about the Steubenville youth conference and thought I'd give it a try.

It was so awesome! During adoration, I experienced such a spiritual healing and renewal. I hadn't felt the love of God in so long. Now I know that everything will be okay. I don't ever want to go back to drugs and sex to fill me because they don't last. Only God does. My heart is so full of joy and peace. My attitude and behavior have totally changed. My life has done a 180 thanks to the grace of God.
Signed,
Rock Bottom

Dear "Rock Bottom,"
When we commit sin, it tears holes in our souls. This makes us feel empty so we try to fill that emptiness with even more things that cause even more holes. We keep turning further and further away from God by creating more and more holes! Now your heart is full of God's peace and joy, and He's the only one that can keep it full. Just keep telling yourself, "No more holes! God makes me full!" (All right, all right. So I won't win a poetry contest...) ✝ Fr. Dave

I grew up in a Catholic family, and I am the youngest of six children. My mother and father are both very religious and taught us all about the church. Yet, I felt as if everything I was told was basically a fairy tale. I didn't believe in God or in Jesus Christ. Actually, I had gone further than not believing in what the Catholic Church teaches. I had become involved in Wicca (witchcraft). I believed in more than one god. I believed in many gods and goddesses. Wicca made sense to me in a way that the church didn't. It was a way for me to solve my problems.

I also got into the party scene where I would get drunk, do drugs, and sleep with guys without thinking twice about it. I got to the point where I didn't want to live anymore because if I wasn't drunk or high, I wasn't happy. So, I tried to kill myself. I took a ton of sleeping pills and slit my wrists. That was my history prior to the Steubenville of the Rockies youth conference.

On Saturday night of the conference when the monstrance was brought out, I was sitting on the side of the gym in the bleachers. The second I saw it, for some reason, I started crying like a baby. I truly couldn't help it! When we were given a few minutes to sit in prayer, I asked God to come into my heart. I told him I was open to hear His words. What went through my head was God saying to me: "Kim, always remember I love you no matter what."

That night after adoration, I went to confession and told the priest everything. He told me I was like a newly baptized child and then said to me: "Kim, always remember that God loves you no matter what." To me, that was like, "Wow!" because I had heard the same

words earlier, and secondly, I hadn't told the priest my name.

That weekend was the best weekend I have ever experienced. For the first time, I truly felt the presence of Jesus Christ, and I accepted Jesus into my heart.
Signed,
Surprised by God

Dear "Surprised by God,"

You are like so many people who think the story of Jesus is like a spiritual fairy tale: It's a great story, maybe even a true story, but it makes no difference in the "real" world. However, like Snow White or Sleeping Beauty, you "woke up" and realized that God is not just a fairy tale, but someone you can experience personally. Because many teens don't know God personally, they get lost in the occult. Please pray for your peers who have been lied to and believe they can find "power" in the occult. The only thing they can find there is darkness, confusion, and death. There is no other God and I am so grateful that you have found Him. This is the "real" world! ✝ Fr. Dave

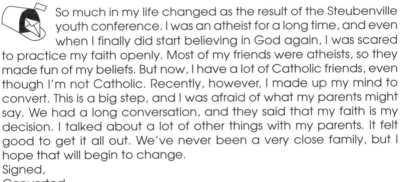

So much in my life changed as the result of the Steubenville youth conference. I was an atheist for a long time, and even when I finally did start believing in God again, I was scared to practice my faith openly. Most of my friends were atheists, so they made fun of my beliefs. But now, I have a lot of Catholic friends, even though I'm not Catholic. Recently, however, I made up my mind to convert. This is a big step, and I was afraid of what my parents might say. We had a long conversation, and they said that my faith is my decision. I talked about a lot of other things with my parents. It felt good to get it all out. We've never been a very close family, but I hope that will begin to change.
Signed,
Converted

Dear "Converted,"

You are quite courageous. You've made the BIG leap from darkness into Light. Stay tight with your Catholic friends. Keep talking with your parents. And keep taking those big leaps of faith. God will always be there to catch you. God has more for you so buckle up. It's going to be a great ride. ✝ Fr. Dave

Before I went to Steubenville in 1998, I was getting in tons of trouble with my family and at school. I had extremely low self esteem and I didn't care what happened to me. My parents argued a lot, which drove me crazy. In addition, I am the middle child, which means that my older and younger sisters got all the attention and I was left to myself.

On Saturday night at the conference while I was crying with my eyes closed, I was slain in the Holy Spirit. I could feel myself being comforted not only by the person holding me, but by the Holy Spirit, the Father, and Jesus. I felt them as a group just hug me. I could feel it throughout my body. It felt so real. The Blessed Trinity was hugging me!

Later, when the monstrance came by, I fell down crying, and cried for a long time. Then I started laughing. That's when I finally lifted my head off the shoulder of the friend who had been comforting me and saw the most amazing thing of my life: Throughout the entire tent there was a bright appearance. I had no doubt what it was. The amazing light was God the Father, His son Jesus, and the Holy Spirit swarming the tent and filling everyone with the glory of the Blessed Trinity, reaching into people's hearts.

The special spiritual high from the conference went on for a few months, but then I began getting in trouble again. I was getting suspended and had many after-school detentions. I lost what I had found because I had let go of it. Slowly, I began to find it again. I began praying more, going to church more, believing more.

When I went to Steubenville for the second time, I refound the spirituality I had lost throughout the year. That Saturday night as the monstrance passed, I cried as I thought of all the sins I had committed, but I knew my heavenly Father forgave me, so I let them go. Then I laughed hysterically. Then I cried a little more as I thought of other things. Then I smiled. I had a dumb grin on my face the rest of the evening. I was filled with energy, strength, courage, happiness, and so much more, but most of all, I was filled with an extraordinary amount of love. That love was God. It was the Father. It was my heavenly Father.
Signed,
Middle Child

Dear "Middle Child,"
You are absolutely right when you say that you lost what you had gained because you let go of it. God is not going to leave us, but often we leave Him. Make sure you continue to pray, spend time with your youth group, and go to Mass so that you don't "lose" what God has given you. ✝ Fr. Dave

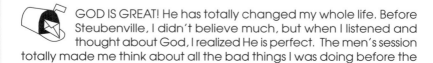 GOD IS GREAT! He has totally changed my whole life. Before Steubenville, I didn't believe much, but when I listened and thought about God, I realized He is perfect. The men's session totally made me think about all the bad things I was doing before the

weekend, and it made me sad because I was terrible. Well, I have to go. I need sleep, so GOD BLESS everyone!
Signed,
Totally Changed

Dear "Totally Changed,"
I hope you slept well. Hey, even if you've done terrible things, that doesn't make you a terrible person. God has forgiven you for everything. Hope you found a priest and made a good confession. It's a great way to start over again. ✝ Fr. Dave

After years of being a "good girl" - good grades, good manners, good friends - I finally snapped. My pent-up frustrations from years of verbal abuse and expectations of perfection at home had to find an outlet. So, I made new friends and did new things. I got drunk, popped pills, and inflicted injuries on my limbs because I felt so ugly and worthless. But Christine, my best friend since kindergarten and one of the best examples of Christ I've ever known, never put me down.

When spring rolled around, several counselors diagnosed me as clinically depressed. Christine invited me to go to an annual youth conference in Steubenville, Ohio. The only options I felt I had were death…or a vacation, so off to Ohio it was.

The first night I stood up for Christ, knowing fully as tears rolled down my face that I meant it. I remember talking to a priest for the first time and confessing my sins and feeling a tremendous peace afterwards even though as a non-Catholic I couldn't receive the sacrament. When I stepped off the bus Sunday night, a deacon, who'd seen the incredible change in me, pulled me aside and said: "This may seem like a complete transformation, but it's only the beginning." Truer words have never been said.

Within a few months, my disabled mother found out she needed another operation just as my father, the only full-time breadwinner of the house, developed macular degeneration and lost his eyesight. As a result, he was laid off and our financial situation became desperate. As an only child, I was suddenly handed far more responsibility than I was ready or even willing to take on. This prompted even more fights, disagreements, and name-calling, but I remained sober, no longer maimed myself, and my depression returned only periodically. My newfound relationship with God had given me hope, but more was needed.

The next summer I attended another Steubenville youth conference and even though the weekend did a lot for me, it lacked the "oomph" of the first year. Then, just as I was about to begin my senior year of high school, my dad was diagnosed with lung cancer.

My mother and I went to the hospital in shifts to avoid each other. Through prayer and the removal of most of his lungs, he lived. That same year, a grade school friend was killed in a car accident, and a friend from one of the Steubenville conferences and a favorite uncle died a week apart. My parents didn't know how to help me cope, and instead, the yelling at home grew worse.

Amazingly, I graduated from high school on time with a decent GPA. When college decision time came around, I shocked everybody, including myself, by giving up a music scholarship in favor of Franciscan University. My lifelong dream was to be a singer, but for once, I decided to put God in charge. The long drive from Massachusetts to Ohio felt like a death sentence. I was leaving behind everything familiar, all my friends, especially Christine.

Freshman year of college was the hardest challenge I'd ever faced. Homesickness, anxiety attacks, and depression were constant burdens. To top it off, God had informed me through prayer that it was time for me to "come home." I'd signed up for the Rite of Christian Initiation of Adults (RCIA) and was to fully enter the Catholic Church that Easter Sunday. I completed the classes...grudgingly.

All I can say is that Easter Sunday 1999 was and always will be the most awesome day of my life. As I stood on the altar shaking like a leaf with my sponsor's hands on my shoulders, I could feel Jesus' triumphant smile. I thought: "I can't believe I almost took my own life when *this* is what He had in store for me."

The strength I received in that moment was immeasurable. This was what my heart had been calling out for all along - to actually receive Jesus in the Eucharist and to receive the Holy Spirit. So many Catholics don't realize the gift they have.

During the 1999 Steubenville East conference, I was the strong one, I was the comforter. No more sobbing outside the tent feeling sorry for myself. On the bus ride home, I proclaimed to the others: "It's not about me anymore; it's about God." I'd finally forgiven my parents for the pain they'd caused me and I understood that they never meant to hurt me. I see what I can and cannot change, and I finally understand that God handles everything for us, if we just give it to Him.
Signed,
Good Girl

Dear "Good Girl,"
Your deacon was correct - your first conference was only the beginning! There was a lot more God wanted (and needed!) to do after your initial conversion. I was so pumped to hear your experience of being confirmed and receiving your first communion. Now you know what the apostles felt. You had your own Pentecost experience. Pray

that others may also have this same experience. God bless you as you continue to find Christ in the Catholic Church and the sacraments. Hope to see you around campus! ✝ Fr. Dave
P.S. You're right - it's not about us, it's all about God!

Prayer

Jesus, thank you for offering your life on the cross for me. May your Holy Spirit come upon me and show me the areas of my life that I try to hide from you. Show me the things in my life that keep me from turning to you. At this moment, I turn from sin and the enticements of the world and turn to you. I believe that you are the only way to Life and I desire to live with you. Come and fill my heart and make yourself real to me so that I may be able to fully give myself to you.

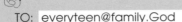

TO: everyteen@family.God

FROM: Father Dave

SUBJECT: **Family**

Family relationships can be the greatest blessing in life. They can also be extremely hard. I mean, relationships with parents can be tough. Maybe you don't get the attention you desire or your parents are negative or always cutting you down. Maybe they don't trust you or never listen to you. Maybe your parents are no longer married. Maybe there's been a death.

All of us want to belong to the perfect family - to have parents who love and care for us; to have brothers and sisters to share the good and bad times with; to have a home that is peaceful and accepting.

There is a perfect family. It's called the Trinity. You never thought of the Trinity as a family? Think about it. The Father, Son, and Holy Spirit love each other perfectly - always patient, always kind, always sacrificing for each other. God designed human families to be a reflection of the divine family, but unfortunately we fall short. We hurt each other. We ignore each other. Sometimes we wish we'd been born into a different family.

The saddest part about an imperfect family is that it affects our relationship with God the Father. If we didn't have a good relationship with our earthly father or if it was non-existent, it can be difficult to approach God as our heavenly Father. But grace can change all that. It can show us that our heavenly Father is there even when our earthly father has been absent. It lets us know that our heavenly Father is patient even when our earthly father has a temper.

Some people (like me, thank God !!!) have been blessed with a great family. We have a wonderful mom and dad, great brothers and sisters, marvelous aunts, uncles, cousins, etc. Some of our greatest memories are from hanging out with the fam, celebrating holidays, and our first trip to the beach!!!!

Yet, even in these family situations, there are hurts. We've hurt our parents and siblings and they've hurt us. Some of my deepest pain comes from my family, and I'm sure that I've caused them pain. (No, I wasn't perfect as a boy...) But that's family - a mixture of love and pain, crosses and resurrections.

But what I want *all* of you to know is that even when family life is hard and hurtful, God has not forgotten you. You are not alone. Jesus came to reveal the Father - not just *His* father, but *Our* Father. The story of the Prodigal Son (Luke 15) tells us that we have a Father who will run to welcome us home. The prophet Isaiah (49:15) says that God will never forget you. Matthew 5 reminds us that God is PERFECT. That doesn't mean just sometimes perfect or most of the time perfect, but always perfect!!!

Yes, sometimes our dads and moms aren't able to love us the way we need. But don't be fooled into thinking God is like that. God's love is the same yesterday, today, and forever. He loves you the way you *need*, not just the way you *want*. His love is perfect. This takes away not only the aching hurt, but in time, it heals our broken hearts.

Your Experiences of Family

WOW!!!!! That's the only way to describe my Steubenville weekend. When we talked Friday night about fathers, I realized how much I missed having one. I've never met my dad, but through that talk and adoration on Saturday I realized how much anger I'd held inside and how many walls I'd built up against God the Father.

I was given the gift of tears during Eucharistic adoration and for awhile, it was sad, but when the band played "When God Ran," my tears became a healing cry. I felt the love of God all around me. I looked around and saw hundreds of other people praising God and feeling His love.

Closer to the end of adoration, I felt an amazing sense of calm and peace. All I'd been holding in was gone, and all I had was love from God and my friends and even people I didn't know.
Signed,
Wow!

Dear "Wow!"
God ran to you! Is there anything greater in life? God loves you so much that He waited on the porch, looking down the dusty road waiting for YOU, His child, to come home. The story of the Prodigal Son (Luke 15) says, "Coming to his senses at last....he set off for his father's house." As soon as we come to our senses, as soon as we are willing to return to the Father and tell Him we have strayed, He ALWAYS runs to meet us and welcomes us home. I think that's so cool! † Fr. Dave

When I was getting ready to go to Steubenville, I was really nervous. I had soccer try-outs coming up and was having lots of trouble with my friends. I didn't want to go, but I thought it would be a good idea to get away from home for a couple days.

On Friday night, when one of the priests said, "Your relationship with God starts with your relationship with your father," I was devastated. My father abandoned me at birth and I had never met him. I don't even know his name or what he looks like. All I could think was, "How can I have a relationship with the Lord when I don't have one with my father?" I was sobbing and couldn't stop.

Our youth director got a priest, and he started to pray over me. I had so much pain, anger, and frustration in me I couldn't handle it. When he started to pray, I started shaking and couldn't stop. I asked the Lord, "Please comfort me. I need you right now." The priest started to pray in tongues, which I had never heard before. It was great.

I was praying my hardest, and I felt the Lord come and comfort me. Once I felt His presence, I was okay. I stopped crying and felt very peaceful. I didn't feel any rage or anger, just peace. It was one of the greatest feelings, and I knew it was Jesus. After that, I could talk about my father freely without feeling anger, without breaking down. I don't feel alone or abandoned any more because I have found the Father, and it's the greatest feeling ever!
Signed,
Not Abandoned

Dear "Not Abandoned,"
"See what love the Father has bestowed on us in letting us be called children of God! Yet that is what we are" (1 John 3:1). Isn't that *RADICAL* - that you can call yourself a child of the living God??!! You have found your heavenly Father, and He has found you. Continue to ask Him to fill the emptiness left by your human father. ✝ Fr. Dave

As a typical Catholic kid, I was raised going to church every Sunday. It was very routine and ritual for me, so I was pretty bored with being "religious." When I was in seventh grade, my parents got divorced. I was relieved because there was a lot less commotion and noise in the house. Five years later, my parents started fighting over custody of me and my sister. It was tearing us apart.

I also went to Catholic school for my whole education. Religion class always presented God and the faith as something impersonal, boring, this-is-the-way-it-has-to-be-and-we-don't-feel-like-telling-you-why type of theory. As a freshman in high school, I started questioning a lot of things and lowered some of my standards. My sophomore year, I heard about Young Life and started going to their meetings. It taught me the basics about the love Jesus has for me and how simple it can be to let Him into your life.

In June 1999, I served as a young apostle for the Steubenville Notre Dame conference. As we were training during the week,

Fr. Dave told us to think about what we thought God looked like. Then, Saturday night, I had a really strong image of my younger sister not being at home when I got there. Keep in mind that my sister and I aren't exactly best friends. She's actually quite annoying.

When the session ended, I ran to the phone to find out about my sister. I made my dad wake her up and tell her I loved her. I guess the feeling of losing her was a wake-up call telling me not to take anyone or anything for granted because it might be gone before I can appreciate it.

So the answer to Fr. Dave's question, What does God look like? is this: God looks like my sister. Like Him, she doesn't do everything I ask her to, but always loves and supports me. Many times what she wants and what I want are two different things. And neither God nor my sister really care about how my hair looks in the morning or how many friends I have. They care about me.
Signed,
Big Sister

Dear "Big Sister,"
Jesus said how we treat the least of our brothers *and sisters* is how we treat him. Sadly, we often treat our own flesh and blood worse than anyone else. I'm so glad you were able to see the face of God in your sister. If we can see God in the people we live with, believe me, we'll treat them very differently. I hope you continue to see God's face in ALL your family and friends. And even when the people who love us fail...remember God won't! ✝ Fr. Dave
P.S. Our sisters must look a lot alike because my sister looks like God too.

The most significant part about my Steubenville experience was being there with my family. All of us were there, and we were able to experience different ways of praising God. The weekend focused on fathers - earthly fathers and our heavenly Father. It made me realize what a wonderful father I have on earth. I now consider myself and my sisters some of the luckiest people in the world.

Adoration and benediction on Saturday night were the most powerful part of the weekend. I cried tears of sorrow, joy, confusion, and relief. After that, I smiled. Everyone was comforted in some way. My father prayed over someone else Saturday night rather than us. He prayed over a guy in our group that needed him more than any of us did. Afterwards when I talked to this guy he said he was happy my dad did that for him.

To sum up the weekend, it was a friendship-making, feeling-finder, wake-up-and-feel-loved kind of weekend. It fulfilled and

relieved my soul. It lifted my spirit and renewed my heart.
Signed,
Daughter of a Wonderful Father

Dear "Daughter,"
You are indeed one of the luckiest (and blessed!) people in the world.
I, too, was raised with a wonderful father, and I continue to thank God
for him. I also pray daily for those who aren't so blessed. Some teens
will go home after experiencing God and will be ridiculed rather than
supported. This totally breaks my heart. Maybe you could join me in
praying for your friends and all young people who don't have the
loving father that you do. Thanks for your prayers. † Fr. Dave

My experience of God was so strong on Saturday. He
touched me in a way that He never did the previous two
times at Steubenville. As I was crying with the gift of tears,
God talked to me and told me that my dad and I are going to be
back together again. My father left me before my first birthday, and I
usually only see him once a year. I had asked God to bring my father
and I together, and He said He would.

What also made me so happy was that the person praying
over me was a lady from Iowa I didn't even know! Jesus had told her
to pray over me. I broke out in tears Sunday before Mass when I heard
that Jesus sent her to me. I was also told that when I received the gift
of tears, everyone from my parish and a couple of other people that
weren't from my parish gathered around me and prayed with me. I
would like to tell everyone about this experience just so that everyone
knows God's love and how God's love can affect people that you
don't even know.
Signed,
So Strong

Dear "So Strong,"
You're right - God's love affects everything. As a young man you realize
the importance your earthly father plays in forming your identity as a
grown man. I'll pray that God reunites you and your father. In the
meantime, look to Jesus and the saints as your role models. † Fr. Dave

The whole week before I went to Steubenville I was whining
and complaining because 100% I did not want to go! I was
pushing myself away from all the God mumbo-jumbo. When
I arrived on Friday, I resisted every attempt to feel God. When one of
the priests asked us to stand up as to what point we were with our
fathers, it brought me to tears. I saw others break down and cry as

well. I had been living in a little world where I was getting along fine with everyone, but it was all made up. This talk made me push past my blind spot and face the bitter reality of how I was living my life.

However, it wasn't until Eucharistic adoration Saturday night that I was able to pull free of some of my restraints. I was singing with everyone when my chest swelled with this overwhelming sadness. I started thinking of all the wrong I have done to Christ, my family, and myself. I sat crying, unable to sing. A picture came into my head of my priest back home, Fr. Martin, sitting Indian-style with me as a little girl in pigtails in his lap. I had hurt myself and was crying. Fr. Martin was holding me as if I was his only precious child and saying to me, "It's all right. Everything will be all right. You'll see. Just wait…"

As my tears subsided, I realized that God had given me a new father - Fr. Martin was now my spiritual father. I suddenly found myself closer to God than I had been 10 minutes before. I started crying again, but this time it was a healing cry. A woman from our core team came over and held me. As she comforted me, it was as if God's presence was pumping through her veins and the energy was radiating into me. I was able to cry even harder and then to be calm. I felt like a vulnerable little girl. God sat right with us and cradled me in His arms.

When Sunday came, I was able to freely show how much I love God. I am still struggling with problems at home and not wanting to admit that I am closer to God, but each new day I push through it and thank God for everything. Now I can come to God for help and raise my hands to Him and say, "Daddy, lift me up; hold me, Daddy!"
Signed,
His Child

Dear "His Child,"
What a wonderful image of God the Father you have given me. If you think about it, this image is at the heart of our faith. God doesn't live in some far-off place, distant from us. No, He came to earth as one of us so He could "sit with us and cradle us in His arms." Amazing! Thanks for your insight! ✝ Fr. Dave

Riding on the bus to Steubenville, I felt like a fish out of water. Everyone seemed so much younger than me. I had been to youth conferences before and for some reason our Lord never seemed to touch me like He would others. I guess there were mainly two reasons why I was going: first, my mom was a youth minister and wanted me to go. And second, because I was going to college in the fall at one of the toughest military schools in the country. I was apprehensive and hoped I would receive some reassurance at Steubenville.

The conference seemed to be going well, but it really wasn't affecting me. I started off Saturday night asking the Lord to be with me. I wanted Him to touch me so that I would know He was truly with me. The procession for the exposition of the Holy Eucharist began. I continued to pray. As the Lord drew near me, I noticed that the Host seemed a brilliant white color rather than the traditional ivory color. I asked the Lord to please touch me. I just wanted to feel His presence. As He passed by, I prayed harder to our Lord and then also to my grandmom and grandpop whom I knew were in heaven. I watched others around me break into tears, some were resting in the Spirit, while I, once again, remained unaffected.

As things began to wind down, my mom turned to me and smiled. Somehow she knew how I was feeling. She came over and stood between me and my brother. She wanted to take a few minutes away from being youth minister to be "mom." We locked arms and continued to sing and worship. Just then a friend came over and joined us. We prayed and my head started to become harder and harder to hold up. My mom noticed this and said, "Jeff, surrender yourself to Jesus. Let go and surrender." At that moment I became totally limp.

In my mind, I started racing through the clouds as if I was on the nose of an airplane soaring. I was going very fast and the clouds were rushing by quickly. All of a sudden, I came to a stop. I looked around and off to my right, standing about ten feet above me in the clouds, was Jesus. I knew it was Him, beyond any question. I could feel His outpouring of love. He stood there with His arms behind His back. He was dressed in a white alb, He had shoulder length brown hair, and His eyes were as blue as the sky. He stood there a moment, smiled, and then He took His right arm and pointed to my left. I looked over and saw my grandfather. He had died 2 1/2 years ago. He always had a big smile, and his smile was the happiest ever. He was wearing a white alb also. He looked much younger and his hair was black instead of the gray when he died. I was so happy to see him. I had missed him so much and now he was standing before me. He never said a word. He kept on smiling.

Then, he turned slightly to his right and from behind him came my grandmom. I was in awe. Grandmom died when I was four years old. I was the first grandchild, and she always loved me so much. Grandmom also looked young. When she died from cancer, her hair had fallen out. Now she had brown hair about shoulder length that seemed to shine as the bright light came through her hair. She was wearing a white alb. I felt so loved and so at peace. They both stood there in the clouds smiling at me. Then, they extended their hands and began to pray over me.

At that moment, I heard the music "The River is Here." That was my favorite song, and I wanted to dance to it with joy. Just then, I began to go back through the clouds and the music became louder.

When I woke up, my mom was kneeling by me with my brother and friend. I began to cry in joy. I could not move. I was cold, and I didn't have any strength to get up. I told Mom that I had seen Jesus, PopPop, and Grandmom. We cried together and Mom continued to pray and praise the Lord. It was a moment in my life that I will never forget. I felt so different. I knew my life would never be the same. I was touched in a way that only a few have ever experienced. If ever I had doubted the presence of the Lord in my life, it was gone.
Signed,
Needing Reassurance

Dear "Needing Reassurance,"
God always seems to know exactly what we need. A couple things about your story were cool. First, you came away knowing God's love and how He is going to take care of you. Also, you realized you are not walking alone. All the saints in heaven are praying for you and rooting you on. We have one BIG family. † Fr. Dave

Prayer
Jesus, at times I love my family and at times they drive me crazy. Why is it that the people closest to me are often the most difficult to love? Lord, be present in my family and bring your grace. Please pour out your love on each and every member of my family. Help the person who is most distant from your love. Help us to love when we need to love and forgive when we need to forgive. St. Joseph, you were entrusted with the care of the Holy Family. Please pray for my family.

TO: everyteen@chastity.God

FROM: Father Dave

SUBJECT: **Chastity**

Have you ever had a conversation about sex with an elderly lady who is hard of hearing while on an airplane? Sounds like the opening line of a joke, but it's not. It's a true situation, and it happened to me. She was a nice lady, and she was intrigued with what I did, so she kept asking: "Do teenagers really show up to these conferences? What happens at them?"

Somehow we got on the topic of sex. (Don't ask me how.) Her opinion was, hey, teens are going to "do it" so why not make sure they have plenty of "protection." She made it sound like you need bodyguards.

I'm afraid many people have this same attitude - teens are going to have sex so at least minimize the "damage." Tell me, how are you going to minimize emotional and spiritual damage? Can we give you a "morning-after pill" to remove the knife in your heart when your boyfriend or girlfriend says they really don't love you? Can we wave a magic wand to restore your virginity and self-respect?

No, we can't, but current movies portraying sex between teens as wonderful and romantic are trying to make you think so. They should keep the film rolling when those same teens end up in my office. They should show them crying as they tell me about the pain and depression caused by an unchaste life.

But movies aren't the only culprits. Our whole culture is trying to tell you that sex is simply about two "consenting" adults. I'm sure you've heard their slogans: "If it feels good, do it." "Freedom is never having to say 'no.'" "You are entitled to sex." Our culture is telling you that if something is available, then you should have it. You're entitled to it. This basically is what the well-intentioned, but horribly mistaken elderly lady was saying to me.

Why is she mistaken? 1) Because sex is not an entitlement, it is a privilege that goes with marriage; and 2) because to say that teens can't control themselves is a lie. Controlling your sexual urges and desires is a decision you make ahead of time. Lying next to your boyfriend or girlfriend without a stitch of clothing on is not the time to discuss chastity. The battle is lost by then. The time to think about chastity is now, when you're not being pressured and your thinking is clear.

So how can we think clearly about chastity? First of all, we have to realize that chastity is much more than "not having sex." You can refrain from sex and still be unchaste by looking at pornography, wearing skimpy clothes, giving in to masturbation, heavy petting, passionate making out, or oral sex. Chastity is an attitude, a way of living. It's not a negative; it's a positive. It's a way of relating to yourself and others. It's recognizing your dignity as a son or daughter of God and respecting the gift of your sexuality. It's a way of honoring God because you honor the way He made you.

Let me tell you a secret: the world doesn't care if you're chaste. In fact, the world doesn't want you to be chaste because then you won't buy its music, watch its movies, or wear certain clothes. But God wants you to be chaste, and it's not because He's a cosmic killjoy. It's because He's a cosmic "thrilljoy." He knows the thrill that comes from true joy rather than instant gratification. He knows the joy and freedom you will experience by being in good healthy relationships where you are treated with respect and dignity. God knows that real intimacy, real love, comes from holy chaste relationships.

If you've lived an unchaste life - either physically or mentally - you need to know that you are forgiven. It's weird, but some teens think that sex is the unforgivable sin. Not true. God loves you and forgives you, and it doesn't matter what you've done.

You also need to know that you can change. You aren't doomed. Your hormones don't determine you. They may rage or make you crazy, but God's grace can handle even your hormones. His grace will help you avoid tempting situations, help you say "no" in the heat of the battle, and even set boundaries before you date.

By God's grace and your wise decisions, you can live a life of purity in body, mind, and spirit. This is the only real "protection" you need.

Your Experiences of Chastity

During the "True Love and Relationships" session at Steubenville West (Arizona), I began to realize how wrong I had been in a past relationship. I had had premarital sex, thinking I loved the guy, he loved me, and we were meant to be. I finally discovered his love was nothing but lust, and I had been pulled in by it. We were together for a year and eight months, and I finally decided the relationship had to stop.

At the session, I realized how sacred sex is. During Eucharistic adoration, I was overcome with extreme guilt and felt ashamed for what I had done. I almost felt as though I wasn't worthy to see the magnificent miracle of Jesus before me. But then, I felt something inside me, as if I had been touched by someone very softly. I realized

God forgave me of my sin, and I felt like I just had to go to a priest and ask that I be given back my virginity. I did just that and felt so new and refreshed. I took the chastity pledge the next day and plan to keep my promise. I know to most people I'm probably not a virgin, but to myself I am because I feel like God has given me a second chance.
Signed,
Second Chance

Dear "Second Chance,"
God has indeed re-created you. Many people believe that once they've made a mistake they might as well keep on making the same mistake. This is crazy. Just because you have made one mistake doesn't mean you are trapped into making the same mistake again. God always allows us to seek forgiveness and start anew. Your experience of feeling ashamed for what you have done and not worthy to be before God is very common. I'm glad that you did not allow that "feeling" to keep you away from His forgiveness and love. ✝ Fr. Dave

I was in a bad relationship for almost three years with someone who was not Catholic and not even a Christian. I realized during the Steubenville West weekend what I've known for awhile - that I needed to end my relationship with him. It was very difficult because I love him, but I know that we were not meant to be together. I need to send my life in a different direction, and I need God to travel with me through life.
Signed,
Different Direction

Dear "Different Direction,"
You've got guts. Ending a relationship that is not leading you to God is one of the hardest things to do. It's also one of the most important. Your boyfriend is supposed to guard your purity, make you a better person, and lead you to heaven. If these aren't his goals for your relationship, something is *seriously* wrong. You deserve to be treated with respect and dignity. Don't fall for someone who does not see your real beauty. ✝ Fr. Dave

When I was in middle school, I fell into sins against chastity. I'll spare the details, but it went on for about 2 1/2 years. I tried to stop, but was unsuccessful until I went to the Steubenville youth conference in 1997.

The first night I was so deeply moved by the talks that I gave my life to Jesus and went to confession. Saturday night, at Eucharistic adoration, I knelt down and stared at the monstrance. I didn't expect anything but a boring evening, but God had other ideas. I suddenly remembered the fact that this WAS Jesus. I found myself shedding a single tear, and before I knew it, I was bawling. But I wasn't sad. No, it was sweet surrender. I looked at the Host and found myself ignoring the monstrance. I went to the Steubenville East conference the next year and had a similar experience.

Then the school year came around, and I fell into sin again. There were even times that, say, I was cutting up a magazine with scissors, and I would look at the scissors and think about suicide.

In 1999, I went to Steubenville again and was changed forever. At the men's session, the speakers asked the participants to share what type of things we struggled with. A sin would be mentioned and then all the guys who had struggled with that sin would raise their hands. I saw that almost everything I was struggling with, every other guy did too.

But there was one thing no one had mentioned - depression and suicide. I raised my hand and was called on. I murmured "depression and suicide." The priest asked me to say it louder. I yelled it out: "depression and suicide." Every guy in the tent was silent, then a number of hands went up. I was not alone.

It was quite a turnaround. I was no longer the unchaste, proud, vain, somewhat suicidal jerk that I had been. I was now a guy who wanted to be a saint. I had spent 20 minutes in confession on Friday. I had wept and laughed with joy at adoration. And I had committed myself to a year of missionary work. I was broken, and God put me back together as a whole new person.
Signed,
A Whole New Person

Dear "New Person,"
Impurity is like a cancer that gets into us and tries to take over. Thank God He removed the "cancer" while you were still young. So many men and women are unfaithful in marriage because they were unfaithful before marriage. If you are called to be married and want to have a successful marriage (and who doesn't), live a chaste life now! ✝ Fr. Dave
P.S. I admire your courage to admit your struggles at the conference. Sometimes just naming and admitting something breaks its hold on us.

I never knew my father because my parents got divorced when I was only a year old. My father never wanted anything to do with me. In elementary school, I had no friends. I went to church with my mom, but I thought it was boring. My mom tried hard to raise me, but she insulted and put me down without even realizing it. I loved my step-dad as my own father, but it just wasn't the same. I tried to kill myself for the first time when I was 11 years old.

Then, I was raped at 13. I had wanted to save myself for someone that I really loved, and since it was gone and there was nothing I could do about it, I started sleeping around. I was introduced to a church youth group, but I was a hypocrite because I went to youth ministry and was still drinking, doing drugs, having sex, and trying to kill myself.

In 1997 I went to the Steubenville youth conference for the first time. I felt the Holy Spirit, but I didn't want to listen to Him. I stopped sleeping around, but I still occasionally had sex. In 1999, I went to Steubenville for the second time, and God touched my life in such a way that I can never explain it fully. I don't do drugs, I don't drink, and I've decided to live out my chastity. I have no more pain because I laid it all at the foot of Jesus' cross and put God first in my life. I know God loves me even though I've done some bad things.
Signed,
At the Foot of the Cross

Dear "At the Foot of the Cross,"
God bless you. I thank God that you found His love and were able to lay your hurt at the foot of the cross. It's the only place to find healing and wholeness when something precious has been taken from you. I hope you are able to look to Mary as your new model of purity and hope. She too experienced great pain and was able to experience Jesus' love at the foot of the cross. † Fr. Dave

Just before I left for the Steubenville youth conference, my girlfriend and I decided that when I got back we would have sex. That conference saved my life, my chastity. It showed me that being a man meant I would wait until marriage, and I remember you saying, "It will be the hardest thing you ever do as a man." It's only Monday morning, and it has been hard already.

When I got home on Sunday afternoon, I went over to my girlfriend's house. Then God spoke through me and I told her that what we had been doing was wrong and that we had to stop. I truly love this young lady and it was so hard to tell her after months of passionate nights that we had to wait. I showed her the chastity pledge, and we talked for four hours. I think we are closer now than ever before. I want her to experience and come to know Christ like I have.
Signed,
Waiting 'Til Marriage

Dear "Waiting 'Til Marriage,"
You made my day! God is going to bless your decision. It's going to be difficult, but doing the right thing often is. You stated that you and your girlfriend are closer now than you have ever been. This is often the case. When relationships are built on Christ, they are so much more real, so much more intimate, and so much more life-giving.
✝ Fr. Dave
P.S. Thanks for being a real man. The world needs more men like you.

Prayer

Lord Jesus, thank you for giving me life and for the many blessings you bestow on me. Father, my sexuality is a gift from you. I am sorry for the times I have not honored you by not honoring my chastity. Help me to understand that sins against chastity hurt not only you, but they hurt me and others. Lord, help me to use every part of my sexuality to bring glory to you and to draw me closer to Your love. It is my desire to be chaste. Please give me the grace to be faithful.

Following Jesus Christ is the most important decision you'll ever make. Of course you'll have to decide whether or not to go to college, what school to attend (Franciscan University - hint, hint!), what to study, who to ask to prom, whether to remain single or marry, and whether you want large fries or a super size, but these decisions aren't even in the same universe as your decision to follow Christ. Your decision to give or withhold your life from Christ WILL affect all your other decisions.

Actually, the decision is pretty simple. If we desire to live forever in heaven, we must choose God. In the Old Testament, God gave His people a choice: "I have set before you life and death....Choose life, then, that you and your descendants may live" (Deuteronomy 30:19). It really is that basic. Following Christ is a choice *for* life. Not following Christ is a choice *for* death.

When Jesus talks about this He speaks of two gates: One gate, He says, is wide. It is easy, many choose it, and it leads to death. The other gate is narrow. It is hard, few find it, and it leads to eternal life. (Matthew 7:13-14) The choice is ours. We must decide.

Just because the choice is simple, doesn't mean it's easy. When I invite people to give their lives to Christ, I *never* tell them it's going to be easy. I've heard people say, "Give your life to Jesus and you won't have any more problems. It will be wonderful...." They make it sound like a walk in the park.

Don't believe them. Following Christ is difficult. That's why many of your stories show how you gave your life to Christ one year and then struggled to keep your commitment. Jesus did not say: "Pick up your skateboard and follow me." Rather, He said, "Pick up your cross and follow me."

Some of you may be thinking: "Dude, what a downer!" No, just honest. For me to say anything else would be a lie. Instead, I want you to know that giving your life to Christ is the only Way. It's the only decision that will give your life eternal meaning, that will bring light out of darkness, order out of chaos. It's the only thing that will bring you deep lasting joy. And the cool thing is that this joy is not only to be experienced in heaven, but it's something God has for us now.

I guess this is the bottom line: Life is difficult no matter what, but following Christ means we don't have to go through it alone. We don't have to carry our cross alone. And don't forget - the cross isn't

the end of the story. There is ALWAYS resurrection if we persevere.

Difficult? Sure. Impossible? No. Worth it? Without a doubt. Read how your peers do it.

Your Experiences of Commitment to Christ

 My life started to change at the Steubenville youth conference Friday night when I stood up and publicly proclaimed that I love Jesus and I am giving my life to Him. I could feel my mind totally free and there was no emptiness inside any more. I was full of joy.

Saturday night changed my life even more! As I was kneeling waiting for the monstrance to come down the aisle beside me, I prayed for the Holy Spirit to come into me and let me be closer to God, closer than ever before. When the monstrance stopped right by me, I felt Jesus embrace me and take away all my problems. I cried and laughed, overwhelmed at being filled with His awesome power.

The thing that puzzled and amazed me is that this wonderful feeling had been there all along, just waiting to be acknowledged. All I had to do was fully give my heart, mind, and soul over to Jesus. Now I can renew my promise to give my life to Jesus every week when I go to Mass and receive His holy body and blood. I will always let Jesus have my life and let Him form it however He wants.
Signed,
Closer Than Before

Dear "Closer,"
Let's talk about close…when you receive Jesus in the Eucharist, you're one flesh with God. It doesn't get any closer than that! Jesus desires to fill you with what you need, to heal you, to be with you. Only He can fill the emptiness of your heart. Once you have experienced this, nothing compares. Keep renewing your promise every week and your relationship with Christ will get stronger. † Fr. Dave
P.S. By the way, Jesus wouldn't mind if you showed up at Mass during the week too!

 When I walked into the gymnasium at Steubenville of the Rockies on Friday night, I couldn't control myself: I started jumping up and down, raising my hands in the air and singing at the top of my lungs. It felt so AWESOME! When it came time for those who had never stood up for God to stand, I began to cry. As I sat there and watched my peers stand, I felt so happy for them. I had done it the year before, and it was their turn now.

When Saturday night came and the monstrance came into

the room, I knelt down. The minute I looked at Jesus I burst into tears. At first I didn't understand why I was crying, but then I realized that I felt at peace. God was with me, and I was asking Him to be with me, to take away my struggles. I wanted to be with Him!!

As I knelt, I began to feel my legs get weak. I couldn't take it. I crumbled into a ball and sat there on the floor and wept. I wept with relief and happiness. That night changed me. I had never opened up to God like that before and it felt soooo good! I didn't want the night to end. I decided I would start all over again and follow in God's footsteps.
Signed,
Deeper into God

Dear "Deeper into God,"
It's hard to stand when the God of all eternity shows up for a visit. It gives new meaning to the Scripture "every knee shall bend," eh? Wasn't it cool watching your friends give their life to Christ? I love it!!! Keep following in God's footsteps and continuing to build this awesome friendship with Christ. ✝ Fr. Dave

 Whoa!! What else can I say?? The Steubenville conference moved me deeply. I now realize that I *do* want to be Catholic instead of Episcopalian.

Earlier in the year, our religion teacher, a Franciscan University alumna, showed our class a video about the summer conferences. I thought it looked lame and stupid, not to mention boring. Then, a devout Catholic friend begged me for three days to go with her. I finally agreed, never missing an opportunity to meet guys since the academy I go to is an all-girls school.

Two weeks before the conference, I tried to kill myself. I tried to slit my wrists. I started seeing a psychologist for my suicidal problem and recurrent depression. Soon, it was the day before the conference, and I didn't want to go. I kept telling myself: "But you don't even believe in God...."

Friday night we checked into our dorm room and I checked out the guys. We went to the tent, and I was frightened more than ever. But then the first talk started. It moved me in a way that nothing else has ever been able to, especially dealing with matters about God. When the speaker asked us to stand up if we wanted to commit our lives to Jesus, I turned to my devout Catholic friend and said, "I can't do this on my own. Would you stand with me?" She agreed, and there I was standing up for Jesus! I couldn't believe it! I couldn't believe myself!

The next two days were two of the best ever in my life. I was committed. I was happy (for once)! I wanted to live and not take my

own life! I only checked out one guy from there on out - Jesus.
Signed,
Standing for Jesus

Dear "Standing for Jesus,"
Whoa!! What else can *I* say?? Your friend knew the truth: Jesus is worth checking out. What a true friend you have! Take a second and pray for your peers who don't have anyone to tell them the truth. I'll pray that you can continue to stand for Jesus even through the hard times.
✝ Fr. Dave
P.S. So you thought the conference looked lame and boring? I'll bet you're singing a different tune now.

The Steubenville youth conference created a drastic change in me and the way I live. All of a sudden I became open to Christ and to what He was telling me. I became aware of all the gifts and the wonders of God, and in doing so set my life free from sin (as much as humanly possible). It was as if a light had been turned on inside of me, and I became someone that I am proud of - all because I became aware that Christ is our Lord and Master and that life with God is much more rich and full of bounty, happiness, and all kinds of health.
Signed,
Drastic Change

Dear "Drastic Change,"
Jesus said that you are the light of the world (Matthew 5:14). He did not say you *may* be the light, you *could* be the light, or you *should* be the light. He said YOU ARE the light. Our world desperately needs the light of Christ that you have experienced. I pray that you'll keep this light burning brightly by talking and listening to God and allowing His Holy Spirit to fill you. ✝ Fr. Dave

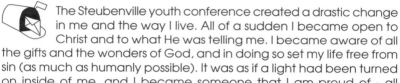

I was a very troubled person before I went to the youth conference at Steubenville. I suffered from clinical depression, drug abuse, my mom having cancer, and more. Friday night a particular song was played and it said to give up your pains. This hit me hard because I have always been afraid of crying. I heard our Lord talk to me and say that He was there and that He loved me. I started crying, something I haven't done in years. When one of the speakers asked those who have never publicly given their hearts to the Lord to stand, I, without even thinking, found myself standing. I cried even more and one of my friends behind me reached out and held me.

During exposition of the Blessed Sacrament on Saturday night, the speaker kept saying to let Jesus into our hearts and let Him take our pains and fears. It was as if he was speaking to me and only me. I had an image in my mind of Jesus sitting in front of me, holding out His hands and asking for my pains and fears. I asked Him to take everything and to fill my heart. I started to bawl. I know it was God's way of letting my pains and fears out.

On Sunday morning, I cried again. I guess Jesus still had some pains to let out. Then I got this amazing rush of heat. I knew it was the Holy Spirit. It was so cool to really feel the Holy Spirit in me. I'm really not sure where I would be if I never had this experience. I might even be dead. I have truly had a victory in Jesus.

Signed,
Giving Everything

Dear "Giving Everything,"
Isn't God astounding! He can take our pains and hurts and transform them. That's the miracle of the cross: God can take something so ugly, so horrific, and use it to bring healing and peace. What seemed to be Satan's greatest victory - Jesus' death on a cross - turned out to be his ultimate defeat. Truly we have victory in the cross of Christ. Thank God that you have experienced this victory. Pray for those who have not been so blessed. ✝ Fr. Dave

Before I attended a Steubenville youth conference, I thought I had a good relationship with God. I had been raised in a loving Catholic family, attended Catholic school my whole life, and was an active member of my youth group. I knew right from wrong and considered myself to be a pretty good person who believed what I had been taught about my faith. I didn't think there was much more to it than that. Did I ever have a lot to learn!

I am very ambitious and had many goals that I was determined to reach. I thought once they were fulfilled, I would be happy. I wanted to be student council president. I worked hard on my campaign and won. I wanted to be Washington County's Junior Miss. It seemed too good to be true, but it happened too. I wanted to buy a new car, have a boyfriend who understood me, and land a good summer job.

All these events transpired. I was happy for awhile, but the novelty wore off and I was soon looking to the next thing to fill the emptiness inside me. I could never be completely satisfied. I didn't understand what was wrong with me. I had everything I wanted and should have been overjoyed, but instead I was overcome with emptiness and a feeling of panic.

I even began to question my future on Broadway. For as long

as I can remember, I've envisioned my name in glamorous Broadway lights, felt the anticipation of opening nights, and craved the applause and recognition of adoring fans. I ate, slept, and breathed theater, dance, music, dress rehearsals, and performances. For the first time, I began to doubt my calling. I wasn't sure of anything anymore and became depressed. I knew something crucial was missing in my life.

My trip to Attleboro, Massachusetts, for Steubenville East was awesome. God worked in me the whole weekend to open my heart to Him. Friday night, I was taken aback by thousands of teens singing and dancing, doing silly motions, and completely letting go of their inhibitions. I thought it was fun, but felt myself holding back.

Gradually, as the songs continued and we listened to wonderful, inspirational speakers, I opened up. I was singing, dancing, and slowly my arms lifted up to God. I wasn't embarrassed or ashamed. I laughed and smiled. I was happy! But this was different. It wasn't the empty happiness of the world. It was the deep, indestructible joy of God. I felt as if I had been dropped on another planet where priests rapped, everyone sang in church, and it was cool to pray. God was the main focus.

I will never forget Saturday night when we all gathered under the tent for adoration of the Blessed Sacrament. I was told Jesus would be present in a special way, but didn't quite know what to expect. Words cannot do justice to the incredible power of the presence of God that night. I was overcome by the awesome love God has for me. My cup overflowed with happiness, wonder, and awe. I felt the Spirit wash over me where I knelt and my head tilted up to the heavens. Nothing existed or mattered but God the Father, Son, and Holy Spirit. My heart beat so fast and my body crumpled beneath me. I lay sobbing on the ground with the realization that Jesus *died for me*!

In that instant, God became more real to me than I ever knew was possible. Suddenly, everything I'd been taught in Sunday school made sense. It was no longer information about some far-off creator. It was the story of my close personal friend and savior. I realized God loves me for me because I am His child. He won't love me any more or less for being student council president or being on the honor roll. In that moment, all the stress, expectations, and concerns of my life were nonexistent and I was free! I was free to forget about rehearsals, dance combinations, and whether or not I would get a lead in the summer musical. A sigh of relief escaped as the drive for success and accomplishments finally relented.

This strange new world consumed the old me. My craving for fame and recognition disappeared. The call of my name in lights seemed empty. I no longer wanted to use my gifts and talents for my own benefit, but for God. The truth of the following scripture passage rings out for me: "But whatever was to my profit I now consider loss for the sake of Christ. What is more, I consider everything a loss compared to the surpassing greatness of knowing Christ Jesus my Lord" (Philippians 3:7-8, New International Version).

I am truly a new person since the Steubenville conference. I possess something deeper than happiness. I overflow with God's joy and I am filled with His peace. I know I am not alone. It's no longer me out to conquer the world. It's me and God working together to spread His love. My priorities have changed and life is much simpler. Of course I still deal with stress, but from a different perspective. I now know that I could work hard my whole life and be very successful in the world's eyes, but without God, my life would have been a failure.
Signed,
Thought I Had It All

Dear "Thought I Had It All,"
In the world's eyes you had it all, but deep down, you knew differently. You kept searching. You kept looking. Your testimony describes the journey of life so well: "Looking for the next thing to fill me." "Overcome with emptiness." "The Spirit washed over me." "Jesus died for me." "God loves me." "Overflow with God's joy." Isn't it amazing what God can do in 44 hours? I'm happy that your name is written in the Book of Life rather than on Broadway. It's permanent! ✝ Fr. Dave.
P.S. I'm sure your talents will be well used for the Kingdom!

Prayer
Lord Jesus, I am sorry for all of my sins. The sin I am most sorry for is _____. Please forgive me so that I may know the power of your love. Thank you for dying on the cross for me. Jesus, I give you my heart and ask you to fill it with your love. I accept you as my Lord and Savior, and I commit my life to you. Fill me with your Holy Spirit that I may continue to have the strength and power to follow you. I love you, Lord.

TO: everyteen@forgiveness.God

FROM: Father Dave

SUBJECT: **Forgiveness**

"It's all about forgiveness." That's a line from an Eagles' song. Uh oh, I'm showing my age. You've probably never been to an Eagles' concert. But that doesn't matter because my point is still the same: It's all about forgiveness.

Forgiveness - we must ask for it and give it. Have you ever noticed how hard it is to say "I'm sorry" and "You're forgiven"? I don't know which one is harder. They're both hard, and they're both essential.

You probably don't remember the '60s movie "A Love Story." Heck, I don't even remember the movie. However, most of you have probably heard the famous saying from this movie: "Love is never having to say you're sorry." Give me a major break! This is one of the stupidest things I have ever heard. To really love is having to say you're sorry whenever you hurt someone or sin against them. And if you're anything like me, that's all too often.

We need to be able to say "I'm sorry," and we need to say it to God first. We can say we're sorry to God anytime we sin. When you blow it, say you're sorry. Ask for forgiveness. Every time you attend Mass you should be saying "I'm sorry" to God. (That's what the "Lord have mercy…" is all about.)

But what really rocks is that God left us a sure-fire way of knowing we're forgiven. We don't have to wonder. We know. It's called the sacrament of reconciliation, a.k.a. "confession." There's nothing tricky about it. You tell God you're sorry, and He forgives you. No catches. No gimmicks. No fine print. Just the pure joy of knowing that you have been given a second chance. Your sins are thrown as far as the east is from the west. Don't ask God about them again because He won't remember.

Now there's only one thing harder than saying "I'm sorry" to God - it's saying "you're forgiven" to each other. This can be really hard. I've prayed with teens who physically shake as they reach the point of forgiving someone who has hurt them. I'm not talking about watching them go to the person and forgive them, but merely getting to the point where they forgive the person in their heart.

Holding anger and bitterness inside of us is one of the most destructive things we can do. If we're not able to forgive, we will never be free. Unforgiveness is like a bungee cord that keeps us from getting anywhere. Imagine for a minute that you're trying to walk away from a person you need to forgive. As you walk away, you're gradually pulled back. The further you get away, the harder it is to walk and the more you are pulled back to whatever caused the pain. It's as if you are connected to that person or event by a bungee cord. Unless you forgive, you will never be free. You will always be pulled back. The hurt and pain will always have a hold on you. You need to cut the bungee cord so that you can walk away. Forgiveness cuts the cord. Forgiveness sets you free.

Forgiveness is an act of the will. It's a decision. We decide to forgive someone. We don't just do it when we feel like it. If that was the case, we often wouldn't forgive. But we make the decision to forgive. Why? Because Jesus has forgiven us. He never asks us to do anything He hasn't already done himself.

One last thought: You also need to forgive yourself. Yep, you need to say, "I forgive me for whatever I did or didn't do." Frequently, when I talk with teens who don't believe they are forgiven, I ask if they have forgiven themselves. I bet you know the answer: A big fat "No." Often this is the first step. We need to forgive ourselves for what we have done so we can cut the bungee cord entangling us. Then we can receive God's forgiveness and experience the freedom He has planned for us since all eternity. Happy cutting!!!

Your Experiences of Forgiveness

When I was 14 years old, I was involved in a very close relationship with a guy. We went out for nine months. In that time, our relationship had evolved into a very sinful one. Yes, that means we had sex. After months of saying we loved each other, he told me he did not want to see me anymore. I was crushed. (By the way, during this time I also drifted further from God and fell further into sin.)

I couldn't handle the fact that my boyfriend broke up with me. I tried everything to get him back. Soon, I started hearing rumors that he was telling everybody that our whole relationship had been a big mistake. I felt as if I could not go on living. I often had suicidal thoughts, very strong ones, and attempted to kill myself twice.

One day a Pentecostal friend invited me to go to her church. I accepted the invitation and there prayed to God to help me get my boyfriend back. At this point, I felt unloved. I felt there was no point in living, nothing to look forward to, he had hurt me so badly. A woman at the Pentecostal church said I needed to ask God for forgiveness, so for 1 1/2 years I prayed for the gift of forgiveness. My heart still felt so empty, so unloved, and I kept looking for it in friends, boyfriends, anywhere I could, and still I didn't find it.

Then my mother paid my way to go to Steubenville West in Arizona. A friend there told me the hardest person to forgive is sometimes ourselves. On Saturday night as the Eucharist went by, I prayed to God and Jesus once more for the gift of forgiveness. For the first time, I was slain in the Spirit. I surrendered my heart to Christ and accepted His love. He gave me the gift of forgiveness that I had been praying for. I felt loved again, and since this time I was looking in the right place, I discovered that all the love I need is found in Jesus Christ. Now I wear a blessed crucifix around my neck at all times to remind me daily that Jesus died for my sins and that I am loved by Him.

Signed,
Got a Reason to Live

Dear "Reason to Live,"
I am amazed at what God has done in your heart. I wish every teen could experience what you have experienced. I wish I could plaster your words on the biggest billboard in the world: "I felt loved again, and this time I was looking in the right place. I discovered that all the love I need is found in Jesus Christ." You'll just have to be a walking billboard for all your friends. ✝ Fr. Dave

 On the morning we were leaving for Steubenville, I woke up really late and my youth group almost left without me. Thankfully, I made it there just five minutes before the vans left.

When we got to Steubenville, people were so nice. They would just come up and talk to us, and ask us where we were from. I thought that was so cool. My favorite part of the entire trip was the Holy Hour, where they brought the Blessed Sacrament and processed through the tent. I noticed that when the monstrance went past people, unusual stuff happened. I saw people crying and laughing out loud for no reason! I guess it was the Holy Spirit filling them with so much joy that they could not contain themselves.

As they were bringing the monstrance down the rows, the priest suggested we reach out and tell Jesus what we wanted Him to do for us. I wasn't exactly sure what was going on, but I reached out my hand and asked Jesus to help me love Him more. I already loved Jesus, but I felt like I wasn't loving Him enough. As the monstrance came by, I felt the strangest feeling I've ever had. It was joy, but also sadness. It felt good though. It was the Holy Spirit. I could feel Him working in me. I started to cry. I didn't even know where the tears came from. All I knew was that they were coming from the Holy Spirit.

It was then that I began to realize that God had forgiven me for all the sins I had committed. Before Steubenville, I felt like I had done so many wrong things so many times that God wouldn't forgive me. I had no idea how much God really loved me. I thought I would never be forgiven.

Then the band played "When God Ran," and it reminded me of my life because I had sinned so much, and when I repented, it was like I was finally coming home. And instead of just me running to God, God ran to me because He was so excited about me coming back to Him! I have never felt so happy in my entire life.

When I got home, I started telling my mom and step-father about my experience, even though they are Protestant. I asked them to come next year. They said they would. Then I went in my room and prayed about my parents becoming Catholic and baptizing my little brother as a Catholic.

I was surprised at the results! A few weeks later, I was talking to my step sister, who was also Protestant, and she said she wanted to become Catholic. I was so excited! My parents also said they were thinking about going through RCIA and becoming Catholic. It was then that I realized my prayers were being answered. My whole family wanted to become Catholic, and we would all be going to the same church instead of always being separated.
Signed,
Forgiven

Dear "Forgiven,"
Isaiah reminds us that even if our sins are as red as scarlet (and believe me, that's red!), we can be washed as white as snow (Isaiah 1:18). It sounds like you got a major bath! I love that squeaky clean feeling my soul gets after I've been forgiven. And you know what? There isn't anything God can't forgive. Even if we wander away from Him, ignore Him, spit on Him, and then realize we can't make it without Him, He's always waiting to welcome us home when we run back to Him.
✝ Fr. Dave
P.S. By the way, welcome home! What an awesome gift to share the fullness of the Catholic faith with your family. They must have seen the change in you and wanted some of what you got...

On the night of July 5, 1996, my grandfather died of a heart attack in my arms. I became very bitter after that and blamed God for my grandfather's death. I wanted to leave the Catholic faith and forget about the church. I tried to find fault with my Catholic faith, and confession, to me, was a pretty big fault. I'd found my reason for leaving and just had to go through with it. That was before my youth director told me about Steubenville Atlanta.

At the conference, the speakers were great and the music was awesome, but I still planned to leave the Catholic Church. Benediction was about to start, so I prayed and asked God to reveal the truth to me. Benediction began and all 1,200 youth fell to their knees in prayer. I closed my eyes and saw a picture of Jesus leaving me and telling me that I do not show Him that I love Him. I broke down in tears and cried for the next 30 minutes. As the priest walked through the congregation with the monstrance, he came toward me and I fell to the ground. I couldn't get up! None of my friends could pick me up, so they prayed over me. It was as if Jesus had put a very heavy cross on my shoulders. When benediction came to a close, I was singing and praising the Lord!

That night, I went to confession for the first time in two years. After I was forgiven of my sins, I felt light as a feather. It felt so wonderful to know that God really did love me, even when I was bitter toward Him. He is always there to welcome us with loving arms.
Signed,
Stayin' Catholic

Dear "Stayin' Catholic,"
Isn't confession amazing? Sin is like a big weight around our necks that pulls us down. When we go to confession, that weight is lifted off us by Jesus, and we really are free - free to be the person we want to be and free to be the person God wants us to be. Thank God for this wonderful sacrament! ✝ Fr. Dave

 The whole conference renewed my precious Catholic faith. Everything about the weekend was great, especially the awesome, fun, faith-filled Bermuda youth group I was with.

The exposition and benediction of our most Holy Eucharist really touched me. It reminded me that the Lord is so loving and forgiving, which brings me to the sacrament of confession. On Friday night, I really wanted to receive our Lord's mercy after the evening session. I went to the chapel and was amazed at how many people were there! I sat down in the last row for about 1 1/2 hours. I watched in amazement as other teens went to confession and came back with tears.

At exactly midnight, I was able to go to confession! I loved how the priest heard my confession, the way he said certain prayers, and went all out. When I received absolution, I smiled and felt the love of the Lord. The priest gave me a hug, and as I embraced him I thought, "This priest is filled with the Holy Spirit and still will be for many more confessions!"
Signed,
Midnight Confession

Dear "Midnight Confession,"
One of the coolest things for me is hearing the confession of teens. There is nothing like looking into their eyes and seeing the love of God being poured into them as they experience God's forgiveness. Thank God for the gift of reconciliation. If you have a second, why don't you say a prayer for all priests that God will bless them as they are celebrating the sacrament of reconciliation. Thanks. ✝ Fr. Dave

Prayer

Jesus, sometimes it is so hard to forgive. Sometimes the hurt is so real and so deep that I don't think I will ever be able to forgive the person who hurt me. Jesus, I can't do this by myself. Send your Holy Spirit to me and shower me with your grace. Help me to see that the reason I can forgive is because you forgive. Come Lord Jesus and set me free. Help me to forgive...

TO: everyteen@loneliness.God

FROM: Father Dave

SUBJECT: **Loneliness and Emptiness**

Here's a happy thought for the day: We are incomplete. There's a hole inside each of us waiting to be filled. Most of our lives are spent trying to fill this hole. Unfortunately, we usually try to cram things into this hole that will never fit. It's like trying to hammer a square peg into a round hole. If you keep hammering, something is going to break. And that something is usually our hearts because we try to fill the hole with things that are destructive, so we end up hurting ourselves in the end.

At times, this hole in our heart makes us feel lonely or empty. This feeling of want, yearning, incompleteness, loneliness - it has many names - can drive us crazy! I remember a teen who told me that he did drugs because it made his emptiness go away. He said he knew it wasn't good for him, but after he did drugs, he didn't feel empty or alone. He was willing to do anything to make that feeling go away. Square peg, round hole!

The hole inside us has a very particular shape. Yup, you guessed it - it's a God-shaped hole. He's the only one that can ever fill it. Oh sure, we try to fill the hole with many things - family, relationships, athletics, school, friends - but we're still empty. All of these things are good, but they're not God. They can never completely fill our emptiness. St. Augustine put it this way: "You made us for yourself, O God, and our hearts are restless until they rest in you." He was a bit more poetic, but it's the same basic point: square peg, round hole. God is the only one who will EVER satisfy the longings of our hearts.

Now permit me for a moment to get on my soapbox and share a pet peeve: There's a difference between *feeling* lonely and *really* being isolated from everyone and everything. The feeling of loneliness is a fact of life. Sometimes, when I come home and check my mail and all I have is airmail (i.e., just air in my mailbox), I feel lonely. I am not really alone. Nothing has changed in my life. I just didn't get mail, and that caused me to *feel* lonely.

God wants to use this feeling of loneliness. If we felt complete all the time, we might think we didn't need anybody or anything (including God). We might begin to think we could live on our own strength or power. We might even feel that we are the center of the universe.

In my life, God has used this feeling of loneliness as an invitation to seek Him. Some of my most profound experiences of God have been when I was feeling lonely. God has used my loneliness to show me that I am NEVER ALONE!!! I could have learned this fact a lot earlier if I had read and believed John 16:32 where Jesus says "Yet, I can never be alone; the Father is with me." Just like Jesus, God is always with me. I may not always feel His presence, but I know He's there. This is the thought I need to plaster across my mirror, bedroom door, and steering wheel: GOD IS ALWAYS WITH ME! Like the air we breathe, I may not be able to see God all the time, but He is constantly filling me up.

Your Experiences of Loneliness and Emptiness

During my sophomore year of high school, I went through 10 months of loneliness, pain, stress, and tears. It was everything combined - school, family, wanting to find a soul mate, my brother disappearing out of my life. Then, something happened. I finally found out what I was missing.

At first, I wasn't exactly liking the idea of praising God in the way they did at the Steubenville youth conference in Attleboro, Massachusetts. But the first night I was there, I broke into tears. I was emotional for no reason, yet it helped me. I knew something was going on inside of me, but I didn't know what.

The second night, my heart started pounding as I listened to the speaker. I started crying like a baby, again, for some unknown reason. Later on, my youth director told me it was God beckoning me and I had to unlock the door to my heart and let Him in. So I did. I let Him in that night, something I had never done.

Now I realize I'm just like any other teenager in the world. There was this feeling inside of me just waiting to come out, burning a hole in me. I no longer have that feeling because I found out what I was missing. I was missing religion. I was missing faith in God, and now that I have found it, I'm forever changed.
Signed,
Found It

Dear "Found It,"
Christ is all about change - taking hearts that are empty, changing them, and making them full. You are correct that you are forever changed. You have opened the door of your heart to Christ, and He will never leave. He's such a gentleman that He will never force His way in. He waits. Knocking, knocking…. I'm glad you let Him in sooner rather than later. ✝ Fr. Dave

I was baptized Catholic when I was little, but never followed the Catholic faith. I was never told to go to church on Sunday, so I never did. When I was about 12 years old, I was reintroduced to my faith through the Big Brother/Big Sister program. Through this program, I met an older lady about the age of 50. She seemed nice, but a bit crazy. She got me involved in a program for adults becoming Catholic, so I received my first communion and was confirmed at Easter 1999.

After first communion and confirmation, I really didn't want to go to church. I hated getting up early and wasn't really interested in God. I fell away from the faith and found myself doing drugs and alcohol. I knew it was wrong, but I didn't care. Life was hard because my mother is an alcoholic and my grandmother yells all the time.

One day, my Big Sister took me to see the Parable Players perform. I had a lot of fun and made a few friends. They were all talking about a place called Steubenville. It sounded boring. One of the women asked if I'd like to go, and I didn't want to be rude and say, "Are you crazy? I don't want to pray for three days straight." So I went.

After a four and a half hour bus ride, we made it to Franciscan University. I didn't want to be there. I wasn't in a happy mood. I wanted to go home. I sat under the big tent and didn't know anyone. The band started to play and everyone was singing and I felt out of place. I didn't know any of the words. I just wanted to go home.

By Saturday, I knew the words to a few songs and was even learning some of the hand movements. I was starting to have fun. Saturday night was benediction and I had no clue as to what it was about. I heard that people start to talk in different languages and stuff, but that was all. A friend I met explained it to me. I thought she was crazy.

Well, at benediction, I started to bawl as soon as they took the Host out of the tabernacle. It felt so good to cry. I felt relieved of all my pain. I knew the Lord was with me and everyone else in the tent. It was great.

Since that moment, I find myself going to church every Sunday and participating in other youth events. God has really filled my life. I no longer feel so empty. Now I realized why I went to Steubenville. God wanted me there, and I am glad He chose me out of millions of children that weren't.
Signed,
Clueless

Dear "Clueless,"
Even though you didn't know what to expect at benediction, God knew exactly what He was going to do. Isn't it great that when we feel

out of control God is still in control? God has a plan for your life. He's been drawing you toward Him through your "Big Sister," RCIA, and the conference. Keep your heart open to Him through prayer, and He will continue leading you. Be sure to pray for the millions who are still looking for what you have found. Many of them are empty just like you were, and they need Christ to fill that emptiness. † Fr. Dave

P.S. I'm impressed that you were able to learn the hand movements to the songs by Saturday. It usually takes me the entire summer.

When the praise and worship started on Saturday night at the conference, I was feeling really down and empty inside. It frustrated me to no end because I had been going after God with my all, pursuing Him with everything I've got for the longest time, and all I had to show for it was the same empty feeling inside. So I started to break down and cry. What made it worse was that the music ministry played a bunch of songs about Jesus being in your heart, and since I felt empty inside, I just cried and cried.

The emptiness seemed to go from bad to worse. But then we sang the song "When God Ran," and part of the refrain said: "He took me in his arm, and held my head to his chest. He said, 'My child, do you know I still love you.'"

After that, I felt like I had been asleep in God's arms, and was having a bad dream. It was the kind of dream where you think your parents have left you, but when you wake up and call out for them, you discover they've been there all along. That's what I had been doing - I had finally "woken up" and Jesus was right there with me. He was reminding me that even when I don't think He is there, He is.
Signed,
Woken Up

Dear "Woken Up,"
Satan's most effective strategy is to make us think we're orphans, that we've been forgotten by God. The truth is, we haven't been forgotten by God, WE'VE BEEN BEGOTTEN BY GOD!! He has created each of us as His sons and daughters. Isaiah 49:15 says that even if a mother could forget her child, the Lord will never forget us. He has engraved us on the palm of His hand. Lock this truth deep within your heart and never give away the key. † Fr. Dave

My whole life I have had at least some kind of relationship with God. In my sophomore year of high school, I became involved with the retreat team at my school. I began to look at others as Christ would, but I still had a sort of emptiness inside.

I wanted so badly for people to believe in the Lord and

surrender their lives to Jesus Christ. I felt as if I was the only person who believed in God and that I was standing completely alone. There was no one my age that saw and believed what I did.

In August of 1999, I attended a high school age youth conference at Steubenville. Words could never express how much it affected my life. I finally wasn't standing alone! There were 2,500 teenagers praising Jesus Christ with me. I was completely overwhelmed with the Holy Spirit and felt at peace in my heart and soul. God finally filled that emptiness in me.

During Eucharistic adoration, I found myself crying, but for what? I wasn't crying for myself. Instead I cried for all those who don't know Christ. I thought about my entire group of friends who are on the path to hell. I wanted them to know that God loves them so much that He gave His only Son so that they could have eternal life in paradise. I cried because my whole life flashed before my eyes and I finally felt whole. I felt like I was hanging on the cross. I could see the nails being driven into Jesus. I could feel His pain in my heart. I never fully comprehended how much Jesus' death meant for me. He died a horrible death; He died so that our sins may be forgiven. It was absolutely amazing. I now know that God put me on earth to be a young apostle, to show God's grace to all who come my way.

The youth conference was the most important, special and exciting moment in MY WHOLE LIFE!!! I wanted to scream to the whole world that Jesus Christ is alive. I want all the non-believers to know that God loves them. I don't have time for all Satan's tricks to mess me up and to prevent me from going to heaven. I really don't care what people think anymore, I am going to my Father's House and I'm going to bring as many people as possible.
Signed,
Goin' Home

Dear "Goin' Home,"
You are not and never will be alone. One of the reasons I collected these stories was so that other teens would know they are not alone. Praise God that you found the right thing to put in the God-shaped hole! ✝ Fr. Dave

Prayer
Jesus, sometimes I feel so alone and so empty that I wonder if anyone really cares, if anyone really notices. Fill up my loneliness and emptiness with your Holy Spirit so that I will be confident that you will never abandon me. Father, even when I am far from you, you run to me. You reveal yourself to me in my darkest moments. Come, take away my fear and despair, and fill me with your Holy Spirit.

TO: everyteen@selfimage.God

FROM: Father Dave

SUBJECT: Self Image

"I look in the mirror and I can't stand what I see. I want to bang my head against it. How can anyone stand looking at me? I am so ugly. How could anyone really love me? I am disgusting."

My heart breaks when I read letters such as this one. Hate is such a strong word that I rarely use it, but unfortunately, many teens hate themselves. This is a tragedy. I wish for one day you could see yourself as God sees you. God sees you as good - not as a mistake, not as worthless, but as good. When God created Adam and Eve, or Rob and Christine, or Mark and Kim, or (put your name here) _____, He looked at YOU and was pleased. He said, "This is good, very good!"

I am a big Calvin and Hobbes fan. Maybe it's because my mom says I was like Calvin growing up. I love the comic where Calvin is standing in front of a full-length mirror in his underwear. He is flexing the very few muscles he has while Hobbes looks on. Calvin, obviously impressed with what he sees states, "Made in God's own image, yes sireee."

Made in God's own image, yes sireee, that's what you and I are. We're stamped with it, branded with it, stuck with it. We can't wash it off or remove it no matter how ugly or ungodlike we may feel. That's what we are.

What does it mean to be made in the image and likeness of God? For eternity, you have been in the mind of God. You were not a mistake. God planned YOUR existence for all time even if you may have been a SURPRISE to others!! (Personally, I love surprises!) God has placed something of Himself in you, a divine spark. Even if you think you've snuffed out the spark, He can still see its glow. God sees you through His eyes, not your own.

Now for the world's perspective: The world is consumed by looks, weight, perfect skin, hair, and clothes. There's a lot of pressure to look a certain way, wear certain things, and have perfect white teeth. The world tells you that your worth is determined by what kind of athlete you are, who your boyfriend is, and what kind of music you listen to. The pressure to fit in is real. One little pimple can bring instant tragedy upon an unsuspecting teen.

Because of the world's idea of value and worth, most teens struggle with their self image. You struggle with accepting who you are, who God has made you to be. Have you ever noticed how we

spend so much time and energy looking at other people and wishing we could be someone else? What a waste of time! Try as you might, you are NEVER going to become someone else. You are YOU. You are a GIFT, one that isn't going to be exchanged or returned. There will never be anyone else like you.

This isn't just feel-good "mumbo jumbo." It's the TRUTH. You have value and dignity and deserve respect by the very fact that you are a creation of God. Your worth isn't determined by how smart you are, how cool your friends are, or whether you look good in a swimsuit. Rather, you have value because God created you and gave you life. You have value because you are a son or daughter of the KING!

I know there are times when you don't feel valuable, when you feel like junk - to be picked up and thrown in the trash pile. Don't even go there! That's when you need your Christian friends (and your Bible) to tell you the truth. Movies, television, magazines, athletes, and other "friends" will tell you that you need to look a certain way to be loved or accepted. Don't believe it. They are not and should not be the source of your identity. They didn't make you. God did, and that's where your value comes from - from the One who made you in His image and likeness.

Your Experiences of Self Image

I am a little overweight and with society the way it is today, it's been hard to be noticed for anything more than being called "fat." So, since I'd been picked on and degraded, I decided I didn't have any reason to live. I have scars all up and down my arm from the physical pain I caused myself as I tried over and over again to rid the emotional pain.

I also have a bad relationship with my dad. He is never home, and he isn't Catholic so it's hard to keep my faith when my parents are a different religion.

When adoration began at the conference, I was filled with the Holy Spirit and started crying. I honestly believe God was holding my hands and heart that night. I'm currently recovering from my problems and am also losing weight. Even though it's hard for me to turn from my human father's grasp, I believe God will help me through. I just wanted to say that if there is someone out there who is doing the same type of thing I was doing or has a similar situation with their father, there is help. Turn to God. He will lead you if you open your heart to Him.
Signed,
In God's Care

Dear "In God's Care,"
You are loved. Don't let anyone tell you differently; don't believe anything differently. Your value is not determined by your dress size or the number on a scale. Many people feel the same thing you felt and are doing the same things you were doing. Please pray that your peers who don't think their life is worth living will experience God's loving presence. Pray that they will be able to open their hearts and turn to God. Pray that God will rescue them like He did you. ✝ Fr. Dave

 I didn't want to go to the Steubenville youth conference because of family problems. Two days before the conference, my parents and I got into a fight. At the time, all I was interested in was ending my life, which a friend and I were planning to do on Friday night. During the bus ride to Steubenville, something told me to wait it out. I don't know who told me this because I had shut God out of my life.

The Friday night session really hit me. It made me realize how negative my relationship was not only with my own father, but also with the heavenly Father. I learned that strengthening my relationship with my own father would also strengthen my relationship with God. This reopened my heart a little to God.

Saturday night the exposition of the Blessed Sacrament opened my heart even more. I was given the gift of tears by the Holy Spirit. The tears made me realize how much junk I was keeping bottled inside. I also realized that to the world, I may be just one person, but to one person I may be the world. This meant I was put on this earth to touch somebody's life. If I killed myself then I wouldn't be able to touch that special person's life. I was also told that I was a precious jewel not only in God's eyes, but in other's eyes as well. This was the most beautiful thing anybody had ever told me. It helped me open my heart even more to let God re-enter my life.
Signed,
Precious Jewel

Dear "Precious Jewel,"
Your story has already touched one person - me - and now it will touch many others. I am so glad God broke into your heart and removed all the junk! He only needs a little opening to enter in and begin the healing. It's amazing how beautiful and special and unique and important we are in the eyes of God. Never forget that. ✝ Fr. Dave

When I started my freshman year of high school, I got off on a great foot. I was very popular. I had so many friends, or at least people who I thought were friends. I was high on life

but in the wrong way. I was constantly lying to my parents, everyone else, and even myself. Eventually, people got tired of me. I was no longer cool. They started to dislike me and eventually I fell into a deep depression. I wouldn't eat. I never slept. I hated everyone because it was everyone else's fault that I hated myself.

I tried to kill myself eleven times. Never once did I come close to finishing. I was too scared. I was afraid of facing God, or not being able to face myself. I only went to church because I was made to go. I felt unworthy, unwanted, and unloved. When I woke up in the morning, I couldn't even look in the mirror I was so disgusted. "You're ugly. You're rude. You're mean. You're a sad excuse for a human..." Those phrases repeated over and over in my mind.

The last time I attempted suicide, I got caught. I wrote a letter to my friend and she gave it to my mother. I got help, but was never fully healed. Things got better until a friend of mine died in an alcohol-related car accident. I blamed myself because he asked me for a ride and I said no. Every night, I had nightmares of him yelling at me for letting him die. I couldn't live with myself. I hated myself and was at the end of my rope when I went to Steubenville West.

Even during the conference the thought of being unworthy and not forgiven stuck in my heart. I went to confession four times, but it didn't seem to help. Then at Eucharistic adoration Saturday night I stopped fighting and just gave in. I remember laying on the floor having a "dream" of Jesus and Satan playing tug of war with my body. I decided to let Jesus win.

I cried and cried and cried. I could feel Jesus holding me like a baby and whispering into my ear, "Everything is going to be all right." After adoration, I felt an overwhelming sense of pure happiness. I ran outside and jumped up and down, screaming at the top of my lungs because I was happy. The feeling of forgiveness and the lack of stress was a great feeling. But what sticks with me most is how warm, comforting, loving, and great Jesus feels while He's holding you.

It has been over two and a half years since my last suicide attempt. It feels great! Now don't get me wrong, all of my problems didn't disappear, but they sure did get a lot easier to deal with. I still fight to stay out of depression, but I know God will never let me fall as long as I'm doing His will.
Signed,
Held by Jesus

Dear "Held by Jesus,"
What a wonderful, beautiful, amazing daughter of God you are! No matter what you think when you look in the mirror, hear the truth of God's love: "You are all beautiful, my beloved, and there is no blemish in you" (Song of Songs 4:7). Hey, why don't you write this on a 3x5 card and stick it on your mirror. That way God can say it to you every

morning! The voices of the world are so loud and so full of lies. Don't listen to them. Instead, fill your mind with the truth of God's Word. † Fr. Dave

The story of my trip to Steubenville isn't full of spectacular events, but when I returned home, I was changed. To begin with, I admitted that my relationship with my father wasn't exactly what you'd call great. Okay, so to be honest, it's nowhere near that. However, I saw it was going to be quite an obstacle to overcome in order to love Christ fully. I decided from that point on I would work even harder to repair that relationship.

Also, before Steubenville whenever I had stood up to rededicate my life to Christ, I had never really, truly meant it. I had done it just because everyone else was doing it. But Friday night when I stood up, I realized I needed to start walking the walk of Christ and not just talking the talk.

I wasn't exactly sure how to go back home and change my life instantly, so I thought confession might help. For the first time in 15 years I really, honestly went to confession. Of course I'd been before, but I'd always told little common sins. I figured that was the easy way to have all my sins forgiven, even those that I was ashamed to admit. I was completely wrong!!! When I went to confession Saturday afternoon and confessed everything, the feeling I got when I finished was incredible. Even though I burst into tears during confession, I came out with one of the biggest smiles across my face and I was truly happy with myself.

Then, I went to the chapel to pray that I would be able to change. But the more I thought about it, the more I realized how hard it was going to be to go home and tell my friends, "I've changed. I don't do that any more." I realized one of the first things I would have to do was get rid of all temptation, which meant throwing out all the alcohol, cigarettes, and drugs, that were in my possession. When that thought crossed my mind, I was like, "Whoa! I don't know if I can do that!"

I tried putting all these thoughts in the back of my head during Eucharistic adoration, but it was impossible. I cried and prayed because I knew Jesus loved me, but also I wondered how someone as great as He is could forgive and love someone like me. Just a few years before I had been suicidal and had plenty of self-esteem problems, to say the least. I realized how I had abandoned God and yet, He didn't abandon me. Even though now I knew that God loved me, I thought about the rest of the world - what will they think of me?

Now that I finally wanted to live like a true Christian, I was scared, even terrified, that I would turn suicidal again because of what others would think. The last few months had been a downhill slide: I

had lost my boyfriend of eight months, started having terrible fights with my family, and turned more to alcohol and artificial things to make me happy. Also, I had lost the pride and self respect I had worked so hard to gain, and I thought if I dedicated my life to Christ I would lose friendships and want to die again.

Then something happened. I had the chance to admit that I had self-esteem problems and be prayed over. I went for it. I stood up, admitting that I had problems while 2,500 youth prayed for me and let me know that God loved me and they believed in me. I finally realized that Jesus really does love and forgive sinners like me.

The first thing I did when I got home was get rid of any temptations in my possession and it felt good. I told my friends I was trying to change. I have support from some and none from others. The ones that don't support me, I pray for them. I now realize it's not what people think of me that matters. The only thing that matters is what I look like in the eyes of Jesus.
Signed,
Walking the Walk

Dear "Walking the Walk,"
You couldn't be more correct. The world is consumed with how a person should look or act. I love the scripture from 1 Samuel 16:7, "Not as man sees does God see, because man sees the appearance but the Lord looks into the heart." In the end, all that matters is how you look in the eyes of Jesus. Scripture says you are the apple of God's eye (Psalm 17:8). He looks on you with delight. He takes pleasure in forgiving sinners like you and me. You were brave to admit you were scared to live a Christian life. A lot of people feel that way because they don't realize how much Christ can help them through His grace. Pray every day for more of it! ✝ Fr. Dave

While on spring break in 1999, I was raped. It was probably the worst thing I will ever have to go through. After it happened, I blamed myself and could not forgive the guy or myself for what happened. I started to deteriorate. I felt worthless and full of shame. My youth minister helped me a lot, but I still couldn't bring myself to forgive the guy.

Soon, I felt the only thing I could control was my weight. I started starving myself. When I would eat, I felt guilty about it and made myself throw up. It was the worst feeling in the world. As for my family, well, I hated to bother them with my problems. My parents and sister don't get along so they have problems of their own. I could never tell my parents what was going on. It would have been such a disappointment.

Then, I went on a Steubenville weekend, and I heard another woman speak about her struggles. I broke down. I felt she knew what I was going through. Then, on Saturday night, I just let everything out - all my anger, sadness, and emptiness. I gave it all to God. Sunday, your homily hit me so hard because it was about the "powerless Christian." WOW! I realized, I'm not the only one who feels that way. A huge part of me was "stolen" the night I was raped and even though I have given it to God, I still feel like that part of me is gone.

Signed,
Powerless Christian

Dear "Powerless Christian,"
You're definitely not alone in your struggles. We all struggle. Some of us are just better at hiding it than others (which isn't necessarily good). Your feeling that a part of you is gone is shared by other women who have been raped. The grief is very deep and very real. To feel whole again will take the work of God. Only He can make you whole again. Make sure you seek out the help that you need. It will take time and prayer, but God wants to give your whole self back to you. I pray He will do just that. ✝ Fr. Dave

Prayer
Jesus, you were sent to earth to show the world the love of the Father. Sometimes I am blinded to my own worth and value. Remove the scales from my eyes and heart so that I may see and love in me what you see and love in me. Help me, Lord, to know and believe that I am your son or daughter, created in your image and likeness. I am precious in your sight. Thank you, Father, for making me.

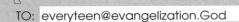

TO: everyteen@evangelization.God

FROM: Father Dave

SUBJECT: **Evangelization**

Hey you! Yes, you, reading this book. Do you realize you're called to be an evangelist? I don't mean one of those preachers on TV in a white polyester suit, but someone who brings the love of God to others in their daily life. Pope John Paul II says *you* are the first evangelizers of other young people - youth evangelizing youth.

You see, in many ways, you're much better equipped for evangelizing teens than I am. When I speak or celebrate Mass, people see my Franciscan habit or priestly vestments and know what to expect (although sometimes I surprise them!). The point is, I'm a priest. People expect me to talk about God. But you, when you speak about God, it's like, whoa... People stop and pay attention. They don't expect it. They're willing to listen. They see your joy and happiness, and they're curious about what you have.

There's an amazing young evangelist in Tyler, Texas. Her name is Jeanne, and I met her at the Alexandria conference. She told me she attended her first conference when she was in eighth grade, and she came by herself. (Hey! Wasn't she supposed to be in ninth grade and come with a group? Hmmm...) Anyway, after the conference she went back to her parish on fire. She told her youth minister about the conference, and she said that lots of teens had to go next year. Her youth minister was not impressed. I'm talking, yawn...ho-hum...I-really-have-too-much-else-to-do....

So, Jeanne decided she would organize a trip the next year. Six people joined her. Not a crowd, but six people is still six people. After that conference, Jeanne again suggested that her youth minister organize a parish expedition for the next year, but still her youth minister refused. Jeanne took up the torch again, and the next year, 30 teens attended the conference, all because she stuck with it and had the guts to act on her convictions. Because she responded to God's call, because she said "yes" to being an evangelist, many teens have heard the good news of Christ and His love.

You've got guts too. I know because I've seen it in your faces. I've seen you stand and make a commitment for Christ when none of your friends were standing. I've seen you give up drinking and drugs even when that meant you would be ridiculed and teased. I've seen you say you're sorry to your parents even when you wanted them to reach out to you first. That's living the gospel. That's being an evangelist.

I remember a retreat I was leading in Colorado. It was Saturday evening and myself and the other adults began a time of worship. Soon, God began to anoint the teens at the retreat. After awhile, all the adults were standing in the back of the room watching the teens minister to each other. I don't think they even realized that we were sitting back watching in awe as God used them to minister to each other. That evening rocked. You have the ability to minister and evangelize your friends. All you have to do is say yes to God.

Your friends need to hear about God's love. They need to know there's another Way. They need you.

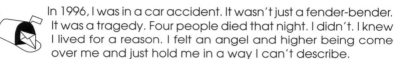

Your Experiences of Evangelization

In 1996, I was in a car accident. It wasn't just a fender-bender. It was a tragedy. Four people died that night. I didn't. I knew I lived for a reason. I felt an angel and higher being come over me and just hold me in a way I can't describe.

Then, on July 17, 1999, at the Steubenville youth conference we prayed before the Blessed Sacrament. For the first time, I was touched by Jesus in a way I have never been touched before. As the monstrance passed by, the band sang "Here I Am, Lord." At that moment, I felt it. I started to shake, then to cry. I cried so hard and for so long. I couldn't stand. I couldn't sing. I just cried, and when I was done, I felt so good. I felt that God and Jesus really do look over me, really do love and forgive all of us.

When I got home, I had a message from a friend, one that I had prayed hard for during benediction. He tries so hard, but he's involved in drugs and gangs, and when I tell him to go to Mass with me, he refuses, saying, "I'm so messed up, I don't even think God will allow me into His house anymore."

When I called him, I told him what happened. I told him that I prayed for him, and when I asked if he was staying out of trouble, he became quiet. He finally told me that he got caught with marijuana and may face up to two years in jail. I could hear in his voice that he wanted help and had nowhere to turn. Getting high is his way of relieving his pain.

But, I know that God has a future for all of us. I know that one of my missions in life is to help this friend, and the youth conference helped me find that out. It helped me find out a lot of stuff. I feel so much purer. I feel so loved, and I have so much love in my heart that I just want to yell and praise God and never stop.
Signed,
Survivor

Dear "Survivor,"
It was no accident that you survived. Your friends are literally dying to know what you know. Look into their eyes. You can see the emptiness. They need to know there is a God who loves them, a God who will forgive them, a God who can give meaning to their lives. You need to tell them. You need to shout it from the rooftops and never stop!
✝ Fr. Dave

 I went to the Steubenville West conference. It was a life-changing experience. I used to think about being a priest or monk, but I always thought it was so boring. But the way you talked about God, your faith was so powerful. I have to go. Talk to you L8er. Bye.
Signed,
L8er

Dear "L8er,"
Priestly life boring? Anything but. Being a priest is the most amazing thing in the world. I believe I am the most blessed person in the universe. I can't imagine doing anything else. I tell students at Franciscan University that I have the greatest job in the world. I get to spend time with young people. I get to invite teens to give their lives to Christ. I get to hear their confessions and celebrate Mass with them. This is the way God has called me to evangelize. Being a priest is UNBELIEVABLE!!!!
Boring? I don't think so… ✝ Fr. Dave

I was so inspired by the Holy Spirit at Steubenville South. Friday night, I could feel the awesome love of Jesus with all 3,000 of us praising Jesus and worshipping His holy name. Confession was extremely spiritual because I knew my soul was clean. Eucharist was from a whole different view as I really knew my Savior, Jesus Christ, was with me. Adoration was so awesome!!! This hour was such a healing time in my life.

Before the conference I'd had a deep faith for about seven months. And now, I know I am called to serve Jesus just like every person is, and I am going to live my life for Christ. I want to be exhausted from serving Jesus on earth so that I just fall into His arms in heaven.
Signed,
Ready to Serve

Dear "Ready to Serve,"
Sounds like a typical weekend for any American teen. (Ya, right…) When 3,000 teens lift their voices in worship of God, the power and

electricity they generate could light up New York City!!! Don't you wish every young person could experience God in this way? Make sure you do your part in sharing what you experienced with others. See you in Jesus' arms in heaven! ✝ Fr. Dave

 At the Steubenville youth conference, I experienced the Blessed Sacrament for the first time, and it was the most beautiful thing. I also received the gift of tears and forgiveness. I loved it so much. I also had the chance to go up to the front when they called for vocations. I would love to become a priest, and I am going to go for it when I get out of school. Thank you again for the experience and everything. I loved it and hope that next year it will get better, but it doesn't need to because it's already perfect.
Signed,
Future Priest

Dear "Future Priest,"
Guess what? Things *will* get better because walking with God gets better and better. Sure there are hard times, but God is always present to carry us through them. I am so glad that you were able to stand at the vocations call. Some people believe there is a vocations crisis. I'm not sure that's true. I think there is a faith crisis. I believe that where the gospel is preached and lived in power vocations will follow. I will pray for you as you continue to seek God and respond to His call. ✝ Fr. Dave

 I just attended the Steubenville conference, and it was truly incredible. I have never felt so close to God. During the Sunday morning session, when we all asked the Holy Spirit to come to us, the speaker said he felt some of us were being called to give a year of their life to Christ as a missionary. I broke down in tears. I believe God is calling me to be a missionary. I have always admired missionaries ever since my field hockey coach went to Mongolia. I will keep praying.
Signed,
Called by God

Dear "Called by God,"
I didn't know field hockey was big in Mongolia. My year with the National Evangelization Teams (NET) was one of the most amazing years of my life. I learned more about God, other people, and myself than I ever thought possible. The church needs young people who are full of energy and zeal to proclaim the saving work of Christ. If you feel God is calling you to missionary work, go for it! ✝ Fr. Dave

Prayer

Jesus, I'm scared. I don't know if I can share you with my friends, my family, or the people at school. I need your Holy Spirit so I will not be afraid. Guide me so I will know what I should do and say. Jesus I trust you will give me the courage and opportunity to share the Father's love with everyone I meet today. Father, someone I meet today will be trapped in darkness. Help me to reveal your light. Help me to be your light.

TO: everyteen@keepburning.God

FROM: Father Dave

SUBJECT: **Keeping the Fire Burning**

How do you keep the fire burning? As most of these stories show, being rocked by God results in change. Many teens decided to end physical relationships, to quit drinking, or to find new friends. However, in time, some of them slipped away from God. Their well-intentioned plans disappeared. When this happens, some teens feel as if God has left them. One teen told me, "Where was God? I felt so close to Him at the conference, but after awhile, it seemed like He was no longer there."

Don't get rattled!! This is a common experience. Every Christian has mountaintop and desert experiences. At times, God feels close. Other times, He feels a million miles away. One time I wrote in my journal, "God, you seem like a stranger I once knew."

So what's up? Does God leave us? Does He move? No. We can't always have this amazing, intimate experience of God. We can't live on the mountaintop, but THAT DOES NOT MEAN GOD IS NOT THERE! God will never abandon you. He will never leave you. Sometimes I have to pray, "God, I don't feel you, but I know you are there."

Are there any survival secrets to life off the mountaintop? Sure, but they're not secrets. You already know them. The most important one is to pray. You must go before God every day and pray. As I was growing up, I prayed every day, even if it was just a simple prayer before bed. Once, when I was a teen, I didn't feel like praying. (Can any of you relate??) I said to God, "I don't feel like praying." To which I heard God say, "And I didn't feel like going to the cross." End of discussion... It's not just about feeling; it's about Truth.

The point is, it's very important for you to communicate with God on a daily basis. You need to spend time with God, just like you would with a new friend. You might want to use the Mass as your model: repentance, praise and worship, scripture, and intercessions. Or you might want to check out the rosary. It's a great way to pray and Mary can help you come closer to her Son. (That's a mother's job, you know.)

You also need to check out the friends you hang with. If your friends are not leading you closer to God, it's going to be very hard to maintain a relationship with Him. Make sure your friends have your best interests at heart and want to help you get to heaven. Also, share with other teens what God has done in your life. It's amazing how God can inflame our hearts when He's the subject of our conversations.

Finally, don't overlook the sacraments. It's essential that you attend Mass on Sunday. ("Remember to keep holy the sabbath day" Exodus 20:8.) You can also attend Mass during the week. There's no greater way to experience His Real Presence than at Mass or through Eucharistic adoration. Several youth groups I know have decided to attend Mass together once during the week. This has been a blessing to the youth group, the teens, and the parish.

You may say, "But Mass is boring at my church." You may not have the music you like, there may not be a lot of teens, but if you have bread, wine, the Word, and a priest, Christ is present. That, my dear friends, is not boring!! And don't forget about confession. It's a great way to remove all the junk that can smother the fire. You'll not only have your sins forgiven, but you'll also receive mucho grace. We can never get enough of that!

Change isn't easy. Persevering is even harder. Sadly, many teens are afraid to go home after a conference or a deep experience of God. They're afraid what they've experienced will be lost or stolen. It's true that things aren't going to be the same and that many teens aren't supported in their faith at home. But what we have to keep in mind is that God can change us. He doesn't have to change everybody else or the circumstances, because He can change us!

After I returned from my year with NET, I was different. God had worked in my life, and my family noticed. One family member said, "Dave is finally the person he has always wanted to be." Exactly! I was free. I was filled with the Holy Spirit. I had received new strength and zeal. I had let the Holy Spirit consume me and set my life on fire. This is the same fire that can keep your heart burning whether you're on the mountaintop or in the valley below.

Your Experiences of Keeping the Fire Burning

I live in a small town that is mostly Catholic, but doesn't live like it. In other words, we are Catholic but don't tell anyone. I had been very strong in my faith until about two years ago when it just wasn't cool. No one shared the same feeling I did, but after the Steubenville conference I came home and shared my faith with one of my friends. He sat and listened to me for two hours! We are becoming closer friends, and now he attends youth group with me and our youth Mass on Saturday nights. It means so much more to me that someone else is also experiencing the faith alongside me.

At the conference, we were challenged to get down on our hands and knees and pray every night, and I am! Before, I never prayed other than at church. Now, I'm praying for other people, things,

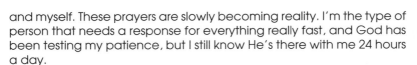

and myself. These prayers are slowly becoming reality. I'm the type of person that needs a response for everything really fast, and God has been testing my patience, but I still know He's there with me 24 hours a day.
Signed,
Sharing My Faith

Dear "Sharing My Faith,"
It's so good to hear that you are praying. If you want to keep the fire alive, you have to "get on your knees and pray." Praying is not easy, and honestly, the evil one doesn't want you to pray. You're going to have all kinds of reasons not to pray and there will always be distractions. Keep trying. You don't have to start big, just start. Talk with God just like you would talk with a friend. The best way to get to know any friend is to spend time with them. God is no exception.
✝ Fr. Dave

 I came to the conference expecting to really light the fire in my soul and to be totally overtaken by the Holy Spirit. I realized that my soul was already on fire for the Lord, but the conference made the fire grow.
Signed,
Overtaken

Dear "Overtaken"
Burn, baby, burn! Let that fire consume you and ignite everything around you. ✝ Fr. Dave

Despite our bus breaking down three times on the way to Steubenville, about 50 of us finally made it to our first youth conference. During the Friday evening session, an altar call was given. I had been at many altar calls. My parents had been involved in the Catholic charismatic renewal since I was around 10. So when I heard the invitation, I thought, "I've already given my life to you, Lord. I don't need to do this."

But God wanted more. He wanted all of me. I'd been feeling that call to "more" for a year and a half. So I looked around at my youth group and realized that none of them were answering the altar call. How could I stand up by myself when none of my friends were? Suddenly, it was as if there was a knife under my chair. I just had to get up and shout my commitment to the Lord. I did what I knew I had to do, and in that moment I felt a freedom I'd never known before. The decision for Christ I'd made a year and a half before had mainly

been a "head" decision. Now, my whole heart was in it too.
Signed,
New Freedom

Dear "New Freedom,"
God does want all of you. For most of us, it's a process to give everything to Him. Each time we respond to God's call, we're able to give a bit more of ourselves. I'm glad you had the courage to stand up and give your heart to the Lord even though your friends were not joining you. It takes courage to live the faith. I have no doubt God will give you all the courage you need. ✝ Fr. Dave

 My story begins in 1997, when as a young 14-year-old, I went to my first conference at Steubenville. I opened up to God, stood up for the first time, made a commitment to Christ, and thought that maybe God wasn't such a bad idea after all.

Freshman year in high school flew by as I grew in my faith. I became active in my high school youth group, liturgical dance, and pro-life projects. I had many ups and downs that year, losing friends, dealing with illness in my family, and the general problems a teen faces. June came around again and I headed for my second Steubenville youth conference.

Braving storms and tornadoes, I witnessed God's power at work and the first of my callings. This calling was to a life of youth ministry and teaching, with missionary work and plenty of God.

Starting school for my sophomore year, I was walking in faith and ready to share it. However, I wasn't prepared for the challenges that were tossed my way. The girls at school ridiculed me and I was teased constantly. But it didn't stop me. I shared my faith experiences and wore a cross with pride.

The year was tough though, and sometime in March it seemed God wasn't really there. I began to replace Him with material things. I was tired of the teasing. I didn't feel accepted anywhere in the world. I became involved in life and lost some of myself. I no longer knew who I was. I was miserable and depressed where there was once a bright and shining light.

I still did God's work but not with as much enthusiasm. God became a burden and Jesus was my cross, one I wanted to give up. Then I became involved with YTM - Youth for the Third Millennium - and got hit smack in the face with myself. Instead of using the voice God gave me for gossip, I started using it for evangelization. Where I thought God had abandoned me, I realized He never left at all.

Then came the best part: my third Steubenville conference. As soon as we arrived on campus, I felt God there again. That night as

I watched my friends commit their lives to Christ, I cried and remembered my own promise to God two years before. I went to confession and the priest told me just to listen, and I did. I listened to everything the speakers had to say on Saturday, and during the Holy Hour, I heard God's voice clearly calling me back to Him. A fire began to burn in my heart, and the burning was an awesome feeling. I let the Lord totally consume me.

Sunday morning, I asked the Spirit to come down on me and He did. My body tingled and burned with the Spirit. I felt God's call again. God asked me to become a missionary, to follow the path I had been walking. I picked up my cross again and knew God's mission was going to be carried out. I can't wait to go back to school to work there as an instrument of God. I've given myself completely to God and now I know my place in the world. I truly feel accepted for who I am.
Signed,
Burning with the Spirit

Dear "Burning with the Spirit,"
It hurts to be teased for your love of God, doesn't it? Others are constantly testing us to see if this "God stuff" is real or just a passing phase. I'm amazed at the strength and courage you have. In classrooms and locker rooms across the country, many teens are living out their faith. These are the real battlefields of today. Don't expect people to stand up and cheer for you. They didn't do that for Jesus, and they won't do it for you. But keep in mind how desperately your school needs the light of Christ and do your best to be that light. Keep the flame alive! † Fr. Dave

I consider June 20, 1999, to be my first day as a Catholic. That was the day God called me back to Catholicism. God is real, and He is inside me now. I am trying to get into my faith more deeply. I have started more serious prayer, and I talk to God more often. I plan to be outgoing with my beliefs and to be an ambassador for Christ.
Signed,
Outgoing

Dear "Outgoing,"
Welcome back to the family! We missed you. I'm sure there are lots of others out there who have strayed away. They need ambassadors like you who will go *to* them and invite them back. † Fr. Dave

I have been to other retreats and youth days, but nothing moved me like Steubenville West. I have never felt so close to Christ nor experienced that kind of love, especially during Eucharistic adoration. I thought I had God in my life, but now I realize I was blocking him out. I have torn down the walls and let Christ in.
Signed,
Moved by the Spirit

Dear "Moved by the Spirit,"
Keep tearing down those walls! So often, we build walls around our hearts because of pain, rejection, and fear. These walls not only keep God out, they also trap things in our hearts that don't belong there. It's great that you were able to let Christ in. ✝ Fr. Dave

August 7, 1999, the "big" Saturday night of the Steubenville youth conference, was my 19th birthday. I couldn't think of a better way to spend my birthday - thanking and praising Jesus directly and in the flesh for creating me. I was so touched.

I felt such a change in my heart as a result of the weekend. God made me realize that I still had His ever-burning fire inside of me, even though I had lost sight of it for a while. Even just thinking about Him makes me want to fall to my knees and thank Him constantly.
Signed,
Ever-Burning Fire

Dear "Ever-Burning Fire,"
"Happy birthday to you. Happy birthday to you..." What a priceless gift you received! God wants to give the same gift of His Real Presence to all of us, not just on our birthdays, but every day! It's a present that never wears out, never gets old, and keeps the faith alive! ✝ Fr. Dave

I accepted Christ into my heart and life for the first time at the 1995 Steubenville youth conference. I went home and drastic changes occurred over the next two years. My entire group of friends changed and my entire life changed. God truly worked wonders in my life even when I didn't deserve it.

Throughout high school, most of my time was devoted to our youth group and I decided in ninth grade that I wanted to be a youth minister and attend Franciscan University. I remained fairly strong in our youth group, working closely with the youth ministers. Then in the summer of 1998, our youth minister moved to California and I was absolutely devastated. In fact, in one month, I lost my youth minister, my boyfriend of over two years, and ten of my closest friends - four of them left for Franciscan University and the others went to various colleges.

I fell into a deep depression. I tried to stay strong in my faith, but I was angry with God because so many of the important people in my life had been taken away. I was confused because God promised that in all our trials we would never be overcome, and I felt overcome. I felt defeated and lost.

Then came the biggest blow of all: My parents informed me that the dream that I had clung to since ninth grade would not happen. They would not allow me to go to Franciscan University. I was at the end of my rope. I had no desire to live, no desire to pray, no desire to do anything but cry. And that I did.

At youth group and church, I did everything I was supposed to do. I went through the motions. I would get into lengthy discussions with people about religion and tell them to accept Christ and all that good stuff, but I was not speaking from the heart. I knew what I was supposed to say so I said it, but I no longer felt it applied to my life.

Then in the summer of 1999, I attended my fifth Steubenville youth conference. As an 18-year-old high school graduate, I felt a bit awkward since most of the conference was geared towards those still in high school. However, something happened to me Saturday night.

While the priest was processing around the tent with the Blessed Sacrament, the speaker was talking about those who were angry or have low self esteem. I started bawling. He asked those people to stand, so I did. This happened just as the priest was walking up our aisle. I was the only one standing in my group and I was right in front. The priest stopped directly in front of me and made the sign of the cross with the monstrance.

To be standing alone in front of the Blessed Sacrament was the most amazing experience I have ever had. I ended up kneeling on the ground, face in the dirt, and crying for so long. During my tears, all the areas of my life in which I had failed my family, friends and especially God were made known to me. God also showed me that the further away I got from Him, the more areas in my life became problematic. It was absolutely amazing and devastating at the same time.

Leaving Sunday I had a new attitude. I didn't really feel anything different, yet something inside of me changed. All I wanted to do when I came home was to fix things. I know it isn't going to be easy, but maybe falling so far away from God after being so close to Him was an important lesson to learn. Maybe next time I'll look back at how bad things got and remember the right way to fix them.
Signed,
Blessed by the Eucharist

Dear "Blessed,"
Through your struggles, you've gained a wisdom far beyond your age. How right you are when you say, "God also showed me that the further away I got from Him, the more areas in my life became problematic." I wonder sometimes why it takes us so long to admit this. Do we have thick heads or what??? Your story also reminds me that life isn't always "hunky-dory" as we continue to follow God. He doesn't always take our crosses away, but He gives us the courage and strength to face them. † Fr. Dave

Prayer

Lord, I know life is going to be hard. You never said it would be easy. Please give me the strength and courage to follow you on the mountaintops and in the valleys. Help me to persevere in the life of grace and the sacraments. You have lit a fire in my soul, and I want it to burn forever. Help me to seek you every day of my life and to follow you wherever you lead.

TO: everyteen@adoration.God

FROM: Father Dave

SUBJECT: **Eucharistic Adoration**

It's so simple it amazes me: Christ promised to be with us always. At Pentecost, He sent His Holy Spirit to fill each of us. But that's not the only way Jesus remains with us. On the night before He died, Jesus took bread, blessed it, broke it, gave it to His disciples and said, "Do this in memory of me." After the meal, He did the same with the cup of wine.

Two thousand years later, we still take bread and wine and remember Jesus. The cool thing is that we're not just remembering an event that happened 2,000 years ago, we're making that event present to us today at every Mass! Jesus remains with us in the Eucharist. It is the Real Presence with a capital "R" and a capital "P" because the bread and wine actually become Jesus. They actually become God!

Does this scramble your brain? It scrambles mine. It's supposed to. It's a mystery. A mystery doesn't mean we can't understand anything about it, but that we can't understand *everything* about it. The one thing we do know is that when the priest prays over the bread and wine, God changes them into the body and blood of Christ. Why does the church do this? Because Jesus told us to: "Do this in memory of me."

However, if you look closely at the bread and wine, you'd say to me, "Fr. Dave, I don't see any change." Bingo! The *appearance* of the bread and wine remains the same while the *substance*, the inner "stuff," changes into the body and blood of Christ. Perhaps the best example to help us grasp what's happening is radiation: If you expose something to radiation, the appearance may not change, but the inside does. That's what makes radiation so dangerous - we can't see the inner change occurring, but it's still happening.

Fortunately, the changing of the bread and wine isn't dangerous. It's life giving. And it happens even though we can't see it. This explains why Mass and Eucharistic adoration can be so powerful. The God of the universe is present with His healing rays. When we look at the monstrance, our human senses see only a round, white wafer, but our spiritual senses suddenly WAKE UP and see the body of Christ!! This can be overwhelming. It can be earth shattering. It can rearrange your universe. It can rock your world.

What's our response to being in the presence of God? Some fall on their faces. Others cry. Others experience forgiveness, cleansing, peace, and comfort. God's healing rays are uniquely designed to reach the depths of each soul and reverse the damage caused by sin and suffering. His presence reminds us that we are loved and that He continually offers us a life of freedom. As you read the following stories, let those healing rays reach you and dismiss any doubt about His Real Presence.

Your Experiences of Eucharistic Adoration

I attended Steubenville of the Rockies, and I am still in complete shock about my experience during the night of Eucharistic adoration. I went into the evening with an open mind and heart, but not expecting anything as emotional and real as I experienced.

When the monstrance was just starting to go around the room, I was praying about my Grandpa McVay who died of cancer not too long ago. I had a fairly close relationship with him and it tore me to pieces when he passed away. I also prayed that I wouldn't focus so much on looks but for my inner beauty to shine. Most importantly, I prayed for the Holy Spirit to find His way into my heart and make me more open to God.

After all of this went through my mind, I realized my whole body was numb. I couldn't feel any part of my body. The tears kept falling and falling, and I couldn't explain why. I was filled with such a joy that I had to cry. Then words started coming into my head. I thought at first I was the one putting these words in my head, but they were coming from my heart. It was God telling me that my grandpa was fine and that he loves me very much. God promised me a better school year this coming year, and He told me that I am beautiful just the way I am.

By this point I was crying so hard it was hard to keep quiet. I have never cried as hard as I did that night. It was a wake-up call to me. I have always known that God was with me, and I have never doubted Him, but I never knew that it was possible to have such a physical experience of God.

I just have to tell you about one more experience I had at Mass on Sunday. I asked God if He would hold my hand. I kept my eyes closed and sang the song the band was playing. All of a sudden, my hand got very warm and it felt as if someone was standing right beside me. As I opened my eyes, I saw my hand curled up as if someone was holding it. I knew right then that God was answering my prayers and showing me how real He is.

Signed,

Holding God's Hand

Dear "Holding God's Hand,"
Yes, God is real. What a wonderful grace you experienced through Christ's presence in the Blessed Sacrament. Sometimes it's hard for us to believe that Jesus is really present. We're similar to Jesus' followers who walked away in disbelief when He said we had to eat His body and drink His blood (see John 6:60-66). That's why we need to pray for more faith - to say to God, "Lord, I do believe. Help my lack of trust!" (Mark 9:24). † Fr. Dave

On Saturday night, as the body of Christ was exposed, everyone in the tent fell to their knees. The focus was on Him, the Son who died for each of us. I blocked everyone and everything out and prayed to God the whole time. I have NEVER been able to do that, but I was SO into prayer that I didn't hear anything going on around me. It was just me and God talking and being father and daughter together. During that time, I argued with God, one of the first times in my whole life. I honestly yelled at God. As soon as God heard my complaint, HE RAN TO ME. And yes, it's hard to understand why some things happen, but He ran to me and I'm trying to run to Him.

I still struggle in my life. Going on retreat doesn't erase all those struggles. It helps us put our hands into our Father's hands and lets Him lead us home. Yes, life can be hard, but please, if anyone else feels this way, know that God RAN. He is an awesome God and He won't leave us alone. He doesn't like seeing us cry and be hurt, but sometimes that's what we need.
Signed,
Honest with God

Dear "Honest with God,"
I am so glad you were able to have an "honest" conversation with God. That's so important. It's funny how we sometimes play games with God. We don't tell him how we really feel, as if we can hide our feelings from Him. However, when *WE* are honest with God, *HE* is able to do more work in our hearts. I can see you've already discovered that. † Fr. Dave

The most anticipated part of the whole weekend was benediction on Saturday night. I still wasn't on an emotional high, and at this point I was beginning to get a little bit bummed. Suddenly, I just couldn't look at Jesus' face. I couldn't. And when He came by me... twice... I reached out and touched His robes, and I broke into tears. I couldn't explain why. It was everything and nothing. It happened twice and I didn't force it.

I don't think I have ever cried so hard in my life. Someone said it was the gift of tears. I didn't know there was such a thing, but I sure am thankful for it!

Well, like I said, I wasn't riding on an emotional high, but I knew spiritually that this was the beginning of my change. Before this had happened, my prayer life was really slipping and so was my spiritual life. The two go hand in hand. I am/was full of selfishness and pride and jealousy, which I threw around in a joking manner. Deep inside of me, though, those feelings were actually taking root and tainting my soul. After this experience, I believe Jesus reached down and pulled me up from sinking in the Galilean Sea and now I'm trying to walk on water and make a difference in someone, anyone's life.

I felt (and still feel) such a peace - a restfulness, peace, and tranquillity. My God is within me. I can't let my fire die again. I have to keep it alive!
Signed,
Reaching Out

Dear "Reaching Out,"
You have learned something very, very important: A relationship with God is not built on just emotion, but on the saving work of Jesus. Then, it is built on _your_ decision to follow Christ no matter what you may be feeling. If we only follow God when we're having a "spiritual high," our relationship with Him is built on sand and the first storm will bring everything crashing in. (See Matthew 7:26-27.) Your enthusiasm for God is infectious! Keep holding God's hand, and you _will_ walk on water!
✝ Fr. Dave

Just before benediction, I decided to walk outside the tent. I was feeling separated from everyone; I felt so different. I didn't even feel human anymore. Looking at God's beautiful sky and all His beautiful people, I felt like a thing that didn't belong, a speck of dust on the picture.

That night I asked God for two things: 1) that He would show me something spectacular during benediction, something I could feel or see to help me believe in what is real; and 2) for God to touch lost souls. I knew so many friends that needed God's touch.

Benediction started and the priest brought out Jesus in His form of simple bread. The priest carried Jesus around and blessed everyone. The priest encouraged letting out what we felt. He somehow explained what I was going through in detail. Christ spoke through him and let me know that I belonged. Christ let me have emotions to show me that I was one of them, and He wouldn't let me forget it. I was around friends. I was around love. I was around deep emotions and spirits. I started to laugh. I couldn't help it - the feeling of belonging was so good and strong in me now. I felt what is called a spiritual high. It not only made my emotions high, but it made my mind clear.

Down a couple seats was a boy who wore a trench coat and his attitude scared some people. He was touched. I saw him cry. I saw him hug the people around him and blow his nose. Everyone felt the change in him. It was real, and it was the most awesome feeling I've ever had.

I realized that God was in me and He was always in me, and He touched a boy that seemed the least likely to be touched.
Signed,
So Real

Dear "So Real,"
God can touch us in the least likely moment, and He can touch the least likely person. He wants us to know that we always have a place in His family, in the church. Even when your parish may not sing the songs you like or be filled with teens on fire for God, Christ is still present in the Eucharist. No matter where you go or where your life leads, He's always waiting in the tabernacle for YOU!! ✝ Fr. Dave

Something awesome happened to me at my Steubenville weekend. Like many other people, it happened during Eucharistic adoration because that's when I was thinking the hardest about Jesus. When the priest came with the monstrance to where I was sitting, I was taken by God. I started praying while a million thoughts raced through my mind. The best thing was that I had gone to reconciliation just before adoration, so I felt truly pure.

I waited for God to take all that I was, and He did. I felt so different after I surrendered to Him. It was the best feeling in the world. I opened my heart, and He came right in. I never want Him to leave. I also have been telling people that I made a new best friend. It was Jesus. He took over everything, and I really talk to Him. He is my best friend forever.
Signed,
Surrendered to Him

Dear "Surrendered to Him,"
Think about it: the Savior of the world, God, the Holy One, Creator of all that is, the Eternal One wants to be our best friend. Talk about hanging out with powerful and popular people! Tell me that's not cool! ✝ Fr. Dave

I never really made a conscious choice to be Catholic. It was just something I always did. When I was a little child, I was very strong in my faith. I knew my catechism and I wanted to be a nun. But as I got older, I lost most of that. Catholicism turned into a Sunday thing that I would do with my family.

That was pretty much the way life was going until Steubenville. I was losing faith daily, my friends weren't that great, and even though I wasn't doing drugs or having sex, I wasn't far from it because a lot of my friends were involved in those things.

My story, though, really starts at the conference. Friday night didn't really affect me because I already have a good relationship with my dad, and the Saturday sessions were good, but the night we had Eucharistic adoration was completely awesome!

At first, when the monstrance was brought out, I was somewhat apathetic because I had been to exposition many times before. But then, when the priest brought the monstrance down among the audience, a friend behind me started crying really, really hard. I was very moved and then I looked at the big wooden cross on the stage. At that point the Holy Spirit really did come into me and I started crying too. I realized so many things about my life, where I was with God, how much He had been present in my life, and how I had so often failed to realize His presence.

And then there was the talk on the prodigal son. I wasn't really the prodigal son; I was more the older brother. I mean, God had been right there my entire life and I was almost oblivious, as if I had never heard of Him before.

So as I knelt on the floor, I cried my eyes out because I thought about how Jesus had died for me and for my sins and I couldn't even follow ten simple rules in return. I thought about how much He had gone through and how much He was hurting on the cross and how every time He had tried to come to me, I had brushed Him away.

The really important thing to me, however, had to do with a decision I had to make. I had to decide whether to go to the public school I went to last year with all my friends or to a new private Catholic school that my brother attended. My parents had left the decision up to me. I had been praying half-heartedly over it, and I wasn't getting any real answers. But then, during Eucharistic adoration, I realized that all along Jesus had been telling me to go to the Catholic school because it would be so much better for me. I realized He had been telling me in the quiet of my heart for so long, and I had completely failed to realize it.

I think that's when I learned about the power of prayer. When I was praying before, I sort of expected a voice to come down from heaven and say, "GO TO MY PRIVATE SCHOOL," or some sort of obvious physical sign. But then I figured out that's not what God does. I really

had to listen, to just shut up and listen to what He was telling me. And I realized that's how God works.
Signed,
Older Son

Dear "Older Son,"
Isn't it cool how God speaks to us? I just love to hear teens tell me how God speaks to them. For some reason, people think God speaks only to "older" people. Wrong. Your story about identifying with the older brother is something a lot of teens can relate to. It's important to remember that God loves both sons the same. It's also important to remember that the older or "good" son didn't go into his Father's house. He was so angry and bitter that he wouldn't join in the celebration. You've got to be really bitter not to attend a party! It reminds me of a quote by Fr. Henri Nouwen: "Sometimes conversion is more difficult if you never leave home." Hey, don't get me wrong. I'm NOT saying you should leave home. It's just that "older sons" have their struggles too. They have to accept the Father's unconditional love just like everyone else. † Fr. Dave

 The second night of the conference, during Eucharistic adoration, I felt the Holy Spirit going through me. Then, all of a sudden, I felt a great feeling go through my body. It made my mind go blank and I felt so relaxed and at peace. Then I became very emotional and started crying. Other teens from different places started to comfort me, and it helped me see that people really can love and that not everyone in this world is violent.
Signed,
Relaxed

Dear "Relaxed,"
Yes, people really can love. What a different world it would be if we were able to really love as God loved. Let's keep trying and never get discouraged. † Fr. Dave

 During the past year, I struggled with my Catholic faith and almost converted to Lutheranism. As the monstrance passed by me at the youth conference, I heard Jesus tell me: "It's me. I am real. Do not be afraid. I exist. This is my church." I have the deepest feeling of Jesus and the Trinity now. I no longer doubt the Eucharist. It is my lifeline, and I will die for it.
Signed,
Eucharistic Lifeline

Dear "Eucharistic Lifeline,"
Amen, Amen, Amen!
You said it all.
✝ Fr. Dave

Prayer

Lord, how awesome is your presence in the Blessed Sacrament. What a tremendous gift you have given to me and the whole world. In the Eucharist, you feed me and fill me with your loving presence. For this I am truly grateful. Help me to believe in your Real Presence even when I'm tempted to doubt. Help me to accept more of the grace you have for me in this wonderful gift. Thank you for waiting for me every day in the tabernacle.

I have read these stories at least 25 times and some still bring tears to my eyes. (I really am very sensitive.) My heart breaks every time I read about a teen who tries to take his or her life. Each time you say you're worthless, I want to look deep into your eyes and tell you of your immeasurable value. I get so frustrated when I see you searching for happiness in places that are going to leave you empty and broken.

So many of you are searching, looking for something to make you feel complete, something to make you whole. You are looking for anything to give your life meaning. You're searching for someone to love you and for someone to love. I wish I could save you from the pain you will experience by giving yourself to another person who won't respect and honor you. So much hurt...

But, of course, this doesn't have to be the end of the story. In the midst of this confusion, God is breaking through. Your stories of victory and triumph give me so much life! I get goose bumps thinking about them. A chill runs down my spine when I hear you talk about coming to know Christ and committing your life to Him. Your stories about forgiveness, wholeness, freedom, healing, mercy, and joy rock my world. So much victory!!!

Please don't stop telling your stories. You live in a world that longs to hear the good news of Jesus Christ. Your peers are dying to hear what you know, to experience what you've experienced. Adults need to know too. Don't ever let anyone look down on you because of your youth!! (Timothy 4:12) God often uses the young to carry out His work - look at King David, the prophet Jeremiah, and Timothy (Paul's companion). Many saints inspired the church by their holiness precisely because they were young: St. Francis started his ministry in his 20s; St. Therese of Lisieux died when she was 24; and St. Bernadette saw Mary when she was a teenager!

In this new millennium, I believe God is sending His anointing on the young. I see a future full of hope and outrageous potential. I see a generation rising from the battle, determined to keep fighting. I see a generation standing tall and shouting out: "ENOUGH! We will not be lied to. We will not be chained to this world. We will not be exploited. We will not stand for sin and death any longer!" I see this generation standing on the rooftops proclaiming: "We belong to Christ." I see a holy generation.